Making Friends with
M U S I C

Making Friends with
MUSIC

James Glennon

Decorations by Val Biro, F.S.I.A.

LONDON
W . FOULSHAM & CO LTD
NEW YORK · TORONTO · CAPE TOWN · SYDNEY

W. FOULSHAM & CO LTD

Yeovil Road, Slough, Bucks, England

For
REX

ISBN 0-572-00774-4

This edition © Copyright James Glennon 1971
Illustrations © Copyright W. Foulsham & Co Ltd 1971

Designed by Rosemary Harley

Made and printed in Great Britain by
C. Tinling & Co Ltd, Prescot and London

Contents

Foreword

My friend James Glennon has chosen exactly the right title for his very interesting and informative book, because when we set out to 'make friends' with music we need just the kind of help he gives us in his well-arranged and very readable little volume.

When, some years ago, I was Deputy Organist of the ancient Cathedral of Winchester I had cause to realise the truth of the old saying 'the eye sees what it brings with it', because it was clear that the people who got most from a visit to that venerable fane were those who had already acquired some knowledge of two things: (a) English history, exemplified in every detail of the building, and (b) Gothic architecture in its various periods.

We shall be very near the truth if we modify that old saying so as to apply it to music and let it read thus — 'the *ear ears* what it brings with it'. In other words, your enjoyment of music will be greatly increased if you take the trouble to absorb the information so clearly set forth in the following pages.

A. E. FLOYD

1

The beginning of music

The first musician was Nature.

Insects hummed and birds sang. The wind sighed from giant trees and ferns. The rain made gentle music as it fell upon rocks and upturned leaves. Water trickled down mountain creeks, and waves gurgled and splashed on beaches of pebbles and sand.

Thunder boomed across the sky. The world became alive with sound.

But, in speaking of early times, when the world was very young and man had no means of writing down his thoughts, we must ask imagination to help us.

Primitive man soon found he could pass on his meaning to others by using the sounds which came from his throat. We can imagine that when he wanted to warn his family of danger he did so by a sudden yell. We can also suppose that ordinary conversation was carried on by a series of grunts, some high, some low, some long, others short.

Gradually he learned to make up words, and so speech began.

Primitive people also found pleasure in a simple form of dancing, making noises as they jumped and whirled about. Because the words which accompanied their dancing sounded better if chanted, singing began.

Then man found he could inspire others with a brave song, or a mother could soothe her child with a gentle, crooning lullaby, and the need came for what we know as music.

The songs of early man would sound strange to our ears today, but in those far-off times they expressed the feelings of these simple people.

As time went on they discovered that other sounds could be made besides those which came from their throats.

From something that began as a means of self-expression gradually developed a form of entertainment for the benefit of others, which became the basis of instrumental and vocal music; ballet, oratorio, and opera.

By stretching the skin of an animal across a hollow log, a coconut or a gourd, man invented what we call a DRUM. This brings us to—

RHYTHM

Have you ever paused to think about rhythm? Our hearts beat rhythmically. Our feet march to it. All creation moves to rhythm; the stars, the tides, the seasons, growth. We shall deal with this more fully in Chapter 6.

ORIGIN OF INSTRUMENTAL MUSIC

Primitive man, besides making drums to beat out the rhythm for his dances, also found he could imitate the sounds of nature. For instance, he discovered that, by twanging tightly-stretched strips of skin, he could imitate the harp-like sounds that came from the vibrations as the wind played through reeds at the water's edge. He learned to make noises which pleased him by blowing into pipes of different kinds.

Even slower than the coming of speech and song into the world was the development of musical instruments.

As time went on, and man found security and pleasure in grouping together in villages, singing provided an outlet for his feelings. It was introduced at feasts, in the market-places and in the home. To add greater variety to the music, more instruments were gradually brought into use.

As the centuries rolled on, early Egyptians and Babylonians learned to blend several instruments together and so the orchestra was born.

The Greeks were somewhat slower in this regard, because they placed great importance on literature and often preferred to listen to the words of eminent writers. The Romans, however, liked to liven up their dinners and festivals by using musical instruments, many of which they invented.

As the chief purpose of this book is to help a fuller appreciation of the music we hear today in our concert halls, on the radio and television, and on the gramophone, it is not necessary to describe ancient instruments and early forms of singing.

2

Musical instruments

Many centuries after primitive man first twanged his crude harp, the LUTE and VIOL came into use. This is what they looked like:

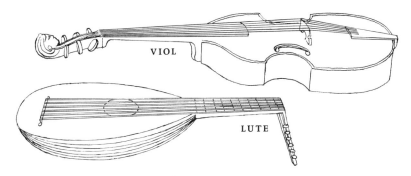

It could be said that the Lute, itself of Oriental origin, was the forerunner of the guitar, harp, banjo and, indeed, all those instruments whose strings were plucked with the fingers. The last use of the lute as an orchestral instrument was about the middle of the 18th century.

STRING FAMILY

As you may have guessed, the Viol was the forerunner of the VIOLIN FAMILY, that is, instruments played with a bow. The viol was first heard in the 15th century and passed out of general use in the 18th.

In the 17th century it became the fashion for families to learn to play various-sized viols and to form small string orchestras. There being no picture theatres, radio or television in those days, people found pleasure in spending their evenings at home in this way. In fact, most of the better-class households of that time possessed a set of viols, usually six in number, of different sizes and musical registers. These were kept in a special wooden chest, often lined with baize, and were known as a chest of viols.

From the viol developed the VIOLIN, VIOLA, 'CELLO and that big fellow, the DOUBLE BASS, all members of the string family that forms such an important part of the orchestra of our time.

The 'cello (the shortened name for violoncello) came into favour about the end of the 17th century, by replacing the VIOL DA GAMBA. This was not so large as the 'cello, but was played in a similar manner. It is quite rare today.

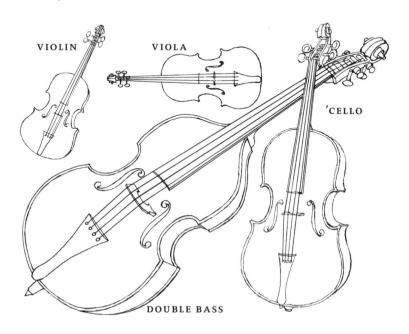

WOODWIND FAMILY

We have already allowed ourselves to imagine that our ancestors long ago discovered they could make pleasant sounds by blowing through a hollow bamboo or reed. The air vibrations within the pipe produced the musical sound which could be altered in pitch by placing fingers over lateral holes.

Members of the woodwind family used in our orchestras are the PICCOLO, FLUTE, OBOE, ENGLISH HORN (COR ANGLAIS), CLARINET, BASSOON and CONTRA BASSOON.

As the RECORDER has been revived during recent years, and is now used in many schools and homes, it may not be out of place to mention this sweet-toned instrument. An early member of the woodwind family, it was commonly used centuries ago in sets of four: descant, treble, tenor and bass. There is a fifth, corresponding to a piccolo and known as the sopranino.

BRASS FAMILY

It is possible that instruments of the brass family had their origin in a large sea shell, the inside hollow of which turns in a spiral, growing larger towards the open end, and in the hunting horn.

From the hunting horn came the TRUMPET. The history of the trumpet goes back to ancient times and we find references to it in the Bible, Homer and other early writers.

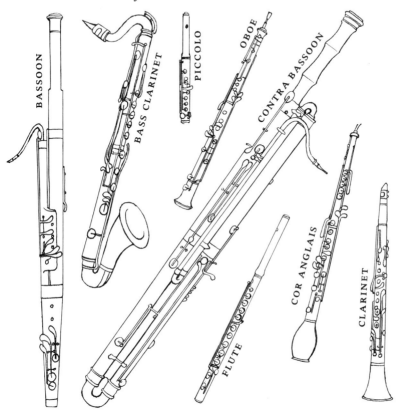

From the trumpet developed the TROMBONE, TUBA and FRENCH HORN. The latter is a kind of link between the woodwind and brass families.

The CORNET, which is somewhat like a trumpet in appearance, is seldom used in modern symphony orchestras but is at home in brass and military bands.

A BRASS BAND is a more familiar sight than an orchestra because it brings its music into the open. As its name suggests, a brass band is made up chiefly of brass instruments: cornets, horns, euphoniums, trombones, clarinets, basses, drums and other percussion instruments.

The MILITARY BAND is a reed and brass-wind combination, and includes instruments found in an orchestra, with the exception of strings, whose place is taken by clarinets. Saxophones and trumpets are also used, and often a string bass. Percussion instruments are also part of its make-up.

There is also the PIPE BAND. Here bagpipes and drums perform the music.

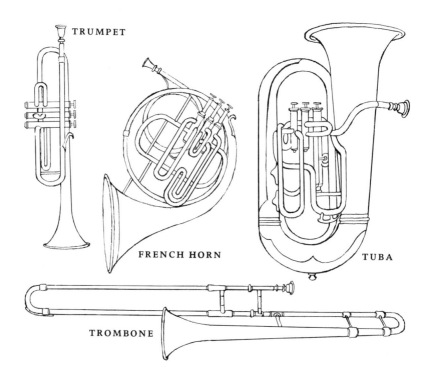

TRUMPET

FRENCH HORN

TUBA

TROMBONE

PERCUSSION FAMILY

In this family (sometimes called the 'kitchen section' of the orchestra) we find the TYMPANI (kettle drum), BASS DRUM, SIDE DRUM, CYMBALS and TRIANGLE. All are hit with wooden or metal sticks, some of which are felt-tipped.

When a composer writers a musical work for an orchestra or band (or a choir), the sheets from which the musicians or singers read their parts is called a SCORE.

In some orchestral scores, composers call for the use of special instruments, or 'effects', such as the HARP, GLOCKENSPIEL (an arrangement of tuned bells on steel bars), TUBULAR BELLS, CHINESE GONG, CASTANETS, TAMBOURINE and XYLOPHONE.

KEYBOARD FAMILY

Everyone knows what a PIANO looks and sounds like, both the grand piano used in concert halls and the upright piano played in homes, but it is interesting to know how this instrument developed.

In the days of Shakespeare and Queen Elizabeth I, the VIRGINAL, a small keyboard instrument placed on a table, was popular. Later came the SPINET (named after the inventor, Giovanni Spinetti), and later still the HARPSICHORD.

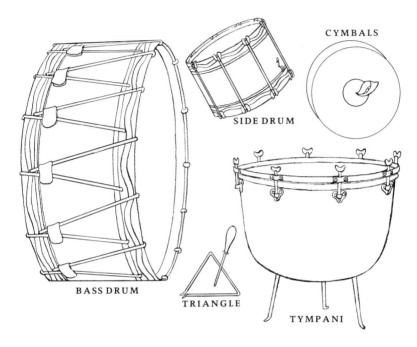

CYMBALS

SIDE DRUM

BASS DRUM

TRIANGLE

TYMPANI

In the early part of 18th century, Bartolomeo Cristofori invented the CLAVIER, which could be played both softly and loudly, or, to use the Italian words, 'piano' and 'forte'. This was the beginning of the PIANOFORTE, known today by the shorter name PIANO.

It will therefore be seen that during the last four hundred years or so many improvements have been made to keyboard instruments and, since Beethoven's time (early nineteenth century) the piano has become an instrument of great power and expression.

THE ORGAN

The ORGAN came into general use early in the Christian Era. It was originally a kind of Pan's pipe, fixed to a pair of bellows. From early

13

pictures we can imagine it to have been a clumsy affair. Improvements were gradually made, but little progress was seen during the first ten centuries of its existence.

In the 7th century, Pope Vitalion introduced the organ into church services to help the singing of the congregation. He probably did this to keep them in tune.

From the 15th century onwards, improvements were made to the keys, pedals, wind-supply and other parts, and in the early part of the 17th century such composers as Bach and Handel made organ music much more beautiful and important.

RELATIONSHIP OF VOICES AND INSTRUMENTS

Suppose one player sounds a note (say, middle C) on a violin, and then players on a trombone and a clarinet sound exactly the same note. The PITCH is the same in all cases, but they sound different. We say they have different SOUND QUALITY, or TONE COLOUR.

Just as the tone colour differs between one instrument and another, so it does between one voice and another, e.g. there are different kinds of sopranos, tenors or basses.

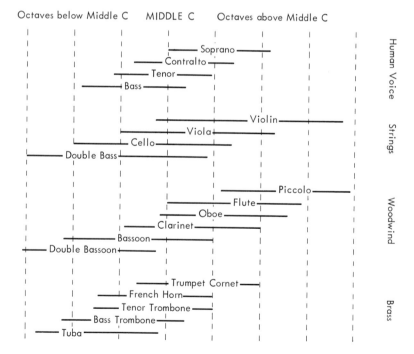

There is another important difference: a woman singing middle C uses a voice an octave (or eight notes) higher than a man singing middle C. So there is a difference in pitch as well as tone colour between women's and men's voices.

Within the range of women's and men's voices there are further divisions: high, medium, and low ranges. A woman's voice can be soprano, mezzo-soprano or contralto; a man's tenor, baritone or bass.

Let us now compare the range of musical instruments with that of the human voice. The relationship is more or less like the diagram opposite.

SUGGESTED RECORDS

HISTORY OF MUSIC IN SOUND (H.M.V.)
THE YOUNG PERSON'S GUIDE TO THE ORCHESTRA (Britten)
LITTLE PRELUDES AND FUGUES (Bach), organ
FUR ELISE (Beethoven), piano
JESU, JOY OF MAN'S DESIRING (Bach), piano
STUDY NO. 12 in C MINOR (Chopin), piano
SONATAS FOR HARPSICHORD (D. Scarlatti)
MEDITATION from 'Thais' (Massenet), violin
THE SWAN (Saint-Saëns), 'cello
ARABESQUE NO. 1 (Debussy), harp
CONCERTO FOR OBOE AND STRINGS (Cimarosa)
FANTASIESTUCKE NO. 1 (Schumann), clarinet
TRUMPET VOLUNTARY (Clarke)
CONCERTO FOR TRUMPET AND ORCHESTRA IN E FLAT (Haydn)
CONCERTO FOR FLUTE AND HARP, K.299 (Mozart)
CONCERTO FOR HORN AND ORCHESTRA, K.417 (Mozart)

3

The orchestra

Let us now consider how the four instrumental families were brought together to form an ORCHESTRA.

On the concert platform we can see these families grouped, all agreeing in a neighbourly, harmonious manner with one object in view—to translate into sound the music which composers have set down in their scores.

But how did the word 'orchestra' come about?

The word itself comes from the Greek, meaning, surprisingly enough, 'a dancing place,' or that part of the early Greek theatre between the stage and the area taken up by the audience. On this space the 'chorus' of about a dozen persons sang or danced, or played their ancient instruments.

In the theatres of today the ORCHESTRA PIT is still between the actors and the audience.

As musical instruments developed and came together in one large family, or group of families, composers wrote special music for them. And so the orchestra took on an importance of its own and played in the concert hall.

In Queen Elizabeth's time (16th century) orchestras contained about a dozen players. Each century that followed saw the addition of more and different instruments.

In the time of Haydn and Mozart (late 18th century) the average orchestra had from thirty-five to forty players. The year 1800 found Beethoven writing for a larger number of orchestral musicians and his music proved to the performers that their instruments were capable of greater scope, or more shades of tone than hitherto. Towards the close of his life (1827) Beethoven wrote his Ninth Symphony and by that time concert-goers were quite accustomed to hearing sixty or more musicians playing together in the one orchestra.

During the early part of the 19th century the French composer Berlioz wrote music for a still larger orchestra. Ten years after the birth of Berlioz, Wagner was born and in time he came to compose orchestral music which called for over a hundred players.

Many of the best symphony orchestras we hear today on gramophone records number from a hundred to a hundred and twenty musicians.

When listening to great orchestras on record, or broadcast, we can find much interest in trying to recognise the various instruments, or at least the instrumental families. It becomes much easier with practice. Now, a word about the SAXOPHONE. Although not usually a part of a symphony orchestra, some composers, chiefly French, have included a part for saxophone in their orchestral scores. It is, however, more often heard in military and dance bands.

The saxophone takes its name from a French instrument-maker, Adolphe Sax, who invented it about 1840, so it is quite a modern instrument.

Orchestral instruments are sometimes used to imitate sounds not associated with the concert hall. For instance, the French composer Saint-Saëns takes us into a zoo in his orchestral suite 'Carnival of the Animals'.

After an introduction, we hear the Royal March of the Lions. This is followed by short sections representing in musical language roosters and hens, the jackass, turtles, elephants, the kangaroo, fish in an aquarium, birds, the swan, and so on. It is quite amusing and also good music.

In his 'Music of Machines', Mossolov, a modern Russian composer, asks the orchestra to make sounds representing a large and busy factory. Another modern, named Honegger, wrote an orchestral piece called 'Pacific 231,' in which he has tried to suggest 'the sensation of hearing a train start up, gather speed and hurl its three hundred tons through the night at a hundred miles an hour'.

We shall read more about this kind of thing in the section 'Programme music' in Chapter 7.

SUGGESTED RECORDS

HISTORY OF MUSIC IN SOUND (H.M.V.)
THE INDIAN QUEEN, Trumpet Overture (*Purcell*)
CONCERTI GROSSI (*Vivaldi*)
SYMPHONY NO. 1 IN D MAJOR (*Haydn*)
SYMPHONY NO. 25, K.183 (*Mozart*)
SYMPHONY NO. 1 IN C MAJOR (*Beethoven*)
BERLIOZ HIGHLIGHTS
CARNIVAL OF THE ANIMALS (*Saint-Saëns*)
RIDE OF THE VALKYRIES (*Wagner*)
1812 OVERTURE (*Tchaikovsky*)

4
Notation

(How musical directions are set down on paper for others to read.)

When someone made up a tune and wished others to sing or play it, it became necessary to arrange a system of writing down music. Just as letters were used as symbols to write down words, other symbols were used to write down tunes. The symbols told the singer or musician what notes to play, how long to hold them, whether the tune should be slow or fast, whether it should be march time, waltz time, and so on.

In other words, a written language for music had to be created, in the same way that early writers invented the Alphabet for writing down the language of speech.

In the 11th century a Benedictine monk named Guido of Arezzo in Italy set out a system of MUSICAL NOTATION. Notes, clefs, bar-lines, sharps and flats and all the other little black symbols we see on music sheets became a musical language.

As an author makes up a story, or a poet creates a poem, a composer not only hears in his mind the sounds and tunes he wishes others to hear, but he must also learn how to write down the notes and other symbols, in somewhat similar manner as an author or poet must know how to set down his story or poem in words. An artist must know how to mix his colours to get effect; the composer must know how to mix his notes and gain the musical effect he wants. In a way, he paints in sound.

Here are some of the more common musical symbols used:

NOTES   CLEFS   BARS   SHARP   FLAT   RESTS

We have now learned that primitive sounds such as grunts or howls developed over a very long period of time into ORDERED SOUND that was not only pleasant to the ear, but also able to convey a musical meaning.

In the Middle Ages most musicians were travelling minstrels. They were regarded as little more than vagabonds or servants. Like Tommy

Tucker, they had to play or sing for their supper. As time went on, music became a respected profession and, later, it was looked upon as part of the training of well-bred men and women.

Man found that music could soothe him, or lift his mind to higher things: that it could help him to think and reason more clearly; that it had the power to stir up courage, or lighten the heart.

Music belongs to everyone. It is a language understood by people all over the world. It is a never-ending source of pleasure, comfort and inspiration. Finding out what the composers intended us to hear is indeed a pleasant study.

We can see rows of print, but we must learn to know what the words mean and what the sentences have to tell us. We can see a picture, but it takes on a greater meaning when we learn *how* to look at it.

We can't all be great musicians, but we can all learn to *appreciate* good music. This can be done by hearing good music in the home or classroom, by listening—really listening—to the works of good composers on the radio and through the many excellent gramophone records available to us, as well as hearing the actual performance in concert halls.

By knowing something about the way music is written down, appreciation of the works of great composers comes nearer to us.

5
Periods of music

We have already found out that music has a history and, like all history, it falls into periods. In some periods, whether it is science, art or music, there is little progress; in some periods there is much.

But composers, like scientists and artists, are always thinking ahead and experimenting, and, therefore, changes are often taking place.

So it has become the habit to speak of the main periods of music:

(1) The music written between the 16th and 18th centuries is usually called CLASSICAL music;

(2) That written in the 19th century is referred to as ROMANTIC music;

(3) That written in our own time is often called MODERN music.

It will be noted that the first period starts from the time when the orchestra and piano began taking the form in which we now know them.

CLASSICAL MUSIC

We are apt to use this term rather loosely, indicating by it a kind of music that is different from the 'popular' music of bands, musical comedy, dance tunes, and jazz. Strictly, the word 'classical' stands for a period. It can also apply to greater literature of the past.

To make this clearer, the term 'classical' is applied to music composed between the end of the 16th and the end of the 18th centuries.

In those times composers wrote music which kept to strict rules of form and to set patterns, rather than intending it should tell a story or paint a scene in sound.

To sum up, the term 'classical' distinguishes a musical work from the 'Romantic' or 'modern'. All this will be clearer as we go along.

ROMANTIC MUSIC

The 'romantic' period in music (also in literature and painting) began in the early part of the 19th century. It started shortly before the time of BEETHOVEN'S death, when composers wished to express human emotions, rather than merely fit their ideas to set forms and models. Although Beethoven built his musical works on standard patterns, he went further along the road of progress than composers before him and introduced a new human quality into his music. So we find in him a link between the classical and romantic periods.

The romantic period (or 'school') in music properly began with SCHUMANN, who painted little scenes, expressed the mood of a poem, and told little stories in music. But the 'framework' on which he built his compositions was the same as that used by earlier composers.

Schumann was joined in this new movement, this new idea of musical expression, by other composers, including CHOPIN and LISZT.

In short, these composers brought out a new kind of music in which the expression of emotion and ideas was just as important as mere form.

MODERN MUSIC

Some people foolishly imagine that no good music has been written since the death of Beethoven. Much 'modern' music may not win lasting fame, but we should try to make friends with it. It may sound unfamiliar, even strange, at first, but we should remember that what may sound uncommon or unusual today may sound quite common and usual in the years to come.

Music, like architecture, writing, painting, motor cars, and aeroplanes, must progress.

The true music-lover must try to appreciate the works of composers of all periods.

When Beethoven's Second Symphony was first heard in 1803, some people described it as the 'cry of a madman'. Someone went as far as to say it reminded him of 'a wounded dragon, lashing its tail about in fury'. Today there is nothing strange about it. We have become accustomed to what was then a new style.

When WAGNER, DEBUSSY and RICHARD STRAUSS (19th century) gave their first compositions to the world, they were described as 'too modern'. Because their style of music was new, some people became quite angry and said nasty things about them. Today we accept them without question.

To define modern music, especially the extreme kind, is not easy. What may sound strange to us is not so much the melodies (tunes) as the unusual harmonies the composer has used. At first, such harmonies (groups of notes sounded at the same time) may surprise us. They may even sound unpleasant at first, but, after hearing them over and over again, we cease to be disturbed by them. We must remember that tunes like 'Rule, Britannia' or 'Waltzing Matilda', or a choir harmonising 'Abide with me', would have been just a jumble of sound to prehistoric man.

Many great composers have been ahead of their time. They wrote music which was not fully appreciated until years later, often after they were dead. The Russian composer TCHAIKOVSKY died in 1893. In his own time some of his music was not completely understood. Today many of his melodies are known to all of us. Office boys whistle them. They have even been 'borrowed' for popular songs and dance tunes. If a musical work is sincere and right, it is likely to last. Time is the test. During the last ten years or so, the gramophone record has brought to light many musical works which, although not accepted when they first appeared, now prove that their composers really knew their job.

To sum up: By the year 1600 the form of choral writing had been perfected by such composers as Palestrina and Byrd. This period saw also the beginning of instrumental music.

By 1750 Purcell, Bach, Handel and other great composers had advanced musical thought and composition.

By 1830 Haydn, Mozart and Beethoven had developed the form and scope of the sonata and the symphony. (More about these later.)

By 1900 certain composers of various nationalities, including Schumann, Weber, Chopin, Liszt, Brahms, Dvorak, Greig, Glinka and Rimsky-Korsakov, had introduced romantic and national expression to music.

Today we find that modern music has been advanced by the experiments in sound of Debussy, Schoenberg, Stravinsky, Prokofieff, Britten and many others.

We shall read more about these composers in Chapter 10.

SUGGESTED RECORDS
Piano

CLASSICAL
    ALLEGRO IN B FLAT, K.3 (*Mozart*)
ROMANTIC
    SCENES FROM CHILDHOOD (*Schumann*)
MODERN
    TOCCATA IN D MINOR, OP. 11 (*Prokofieff*)

Songs

CLASSICAL
    NYMPHS AND SHEPHERDS (*Purcell*)
    NON TEMER, AMATO BENE, K.490 (*Mozart*)
ROMANTIC
    ON WINGS OF SONG (*Mendelssohn*)
    LULLABY (*Brahms*)
MODERN
    SILENT NOON (*Vaughan Williams*)
    A SHROPSHIRE LAD song cycle (*Butterworth*)

6
How musical works are built

All of us, unless completely tone deaf, can follow a simple tune. Even a young child can recognise 'Twinkle, Twinkle, Little Star' or 'God Save the Queen'.

Music can be understood by people in various parts of the world, although there are certain differences between the music of one nation and another, just as there are different dialects in speech.

In such countries as England, France, Germany, Italy, Spain, Poland, Russia, and Australia, the basis of musical expression and the system of notation are much the same. The music varies only in the way that the style of buildings, paintings or dress may vary from one country to another.

Oriental music (for instance, that of China and Japan) is built differently. That is why music from those parts may sound strange to us and ours may sound strange to them. Hindu music makes use of sixty-three different scales, which is many more than other countries use.

SCALES

The word 'scale' comes from the Latin and Italian word *'scala'* meaning 'ladder'. A scale is therefore a climbing succession of notes. The notes are arranged in alphabetical order. This is what a scale looks like on paper:

A scale can be made to start from any note and gets its name from the starting note, such as scale of C, scale of G.

MELODY

It might be said that the melody in music is like the story or theme in literature. It is the tune; in other words, a series of sounds with a definite form, some notes higher or lower than the others, some of them longer or shorter than their companions.

Some melodies complete themselves within a few notes, while others may stretch themselves over several bars. (We'll read about bar-lines further on.)

Take, for instance, 'Rule, Britannia'. Here we can catch the melody (or tune) within the first few notes. In some compositions (as in the case of some of Wagner's music) we might wait for several bars before the melody is complete.

Some musical works have more than one melody.

Next time you hear a piece of orchestral music, say a symphony, try to pick out the principal melody and follow its course, just as you would follow a major river on a map. You'll find this can be quite interesting. In looking at a map, you will notice that a river will follow a certain course, while receiving branches from other directions. These branches, as you know, are called tributaries.

So a melody may thread its way through a musical work and from it may spring other melodies. These we could call tributary melodies.

VARIATIONS

Many composers have taken a tune, lasting perhaps only half a minute or so, used it at the beginning as a THEME and have built a series of VARIATIONS on it. Throughout the work, lasting anything from ten to thirty minutes, we can hear this tune (or theme) repeated over and over again, but given a different rhythm (or time), or a new musical colour, every time it appears. Although the melody takes on a different shape, or character, each time, it is always there.

One of the six hundred songs composed by Schubert is called 'The Trout'. He must have liked the melody very much, for in later years, at the suggestion of some of his friends, he wrote a quintet for piano and four stringed instruments, taking the tune he had used in the song and treating it in six different ways. This is usually known as the 'Trout' Quintet.

Many other composers have written fine music in this way. Someone once wrote a series of variations on that simple melody 'Nellie Bly' and whilst each variation called for a new rhythm, different times (slow and quick) and different combinations of instruments, the tune was never lost.

RHYTHM

We have already spoken of rhythm. But what exactly is it?

We might say that rhythm is to music what the heartbeat is to life. Rhythm in music is like the metre in verse. There is rhythm in marching feet, the sound of train wheels in motion, the ticking of a clock. It is the regularity of the swing that gives the rhythm. Although it is a kind of time pattern, time and rhythm are not quite the same thing. Time is shown as an arrangement of BEATS by figures on the left-hand side of a line of music: for instance, 2/4, 3/4, 4/4, 6/8, etc. Rhythm, however, is the PULSE of music.

Just as the writer uses punctuation, so the composer uses BAR-LINES. These divide the music into regular sections. (See Chapter 4.)

But to return to rhythm. A waltz and a mazurka are both written in 3/4 time, but the rhythms of the two are distinct. A movement from a Beethoven symphony may be written in the same time as the latest popular song, but the rhythm may be entirely different. An Irish reel, a Spanish dance and a modern dance tune might all be written in the same time, but each has its own rhythmic pattern, or pulse.

Without rhythm a musical phrase would be lifeless.

HARMONY

For many centuries after people first found pleasure in singing together, they sang in unison. That is to say, they all sang the same notes. When people first formed choirs, as in the early churches, they still sang in unison. A certain variety of tone was obtained because boys and women sang an octave (or full scale) higher than the men. But they still sang a single line of melody; the same notes and tune.

By the 10th century it was found that still greater variety could be gained by some voices singing in other intervals than a full scale or octave. They sang other notes that blended and which, therefore, sounded pleasant to the ear. Although they all sang the same melody together, it was found that, by several parts of the choir singing different intervals, there was less monotony and a more colourful effect was achieved.

This was the beginning of HARMONY, or chords.

Much more pleasing to the ear is this chord (an harmonic arrangement of notes): than this:

The first is a chord, the second only the same note sounded an octave higher.

Now, let us look at the example on the next page.

You will see by the words that here we have the first two bars of the National Anthem 'God Save the Queen'. Reading from the left, first is the treble clef, then the symbol for a sharp, in this case F sharp, which denotes the key. The 3/4 sign indicates the time in which we should play it, in other words, three beats to the bar. Then follows three chords, then a bar-line. And so on. The top line is played on the piano by the right hand, the bottom line by the left hand, but here we have the bass clef instead of the treble clef.

The top line of notes give us the melody. The notes underneath, all

played together, give the melody a richer sound. This is what we mean by harmony.

SUGGESTED RECORDS

MELODY
SONG WITHOUT WORDS, Op. 19, No. 1 (*Mendelssohn*), piano
HARMONY
PRELUDE IN C MINOR, Op. 28, No. 20 (*Chopin*), piano
VARIATIONS
ABEGG, Theme and Variations (*Schumann*)
RHYTHM
POLONAISES Nos. 1 and 6 (*Chopin*), piano
WEDDING DAY AT TROLDHAUGEN (*Grieg*), piano.
MUSIC FROM SPAIN (*Albeniz, Falla* or *Granados*)

7

Types of music

(a) ORATORIO

Because vocal music developed earlier than instrumental music, let us start with ORATORIO.

The word itself derives from the Latin word 'to speak'.

Two of the best-known oratorios today are Handel's 'Messiah' and Mendelssohn's 'Elijah'. If you are fortunate enough to have been present at performances of these great works, you will know that the music is sung by a choir, and by solo voices, with an orchestral accompaniment. In the case of performances given in a church, the accompaniment is often played on the organ.

Oratorio is different from opera and calls for no scenery, costumes or action.

How did oratorio begin?

During the 14th and 15th centuries, stories from the Old and New Testaments were recited and sung. This made their meaning clearer to the people.

In the 16th century an Italian priest named Philip Neri broadened this idea and introduced a more 'popular' form of church service. For this purpose Father Neri used a building called oratory. This led to his forming, in Rome, a religious order known as the Congregation of Oratorians. After the death of Father Neri in 1595 (he was canonized Saint Philip in 1622), this practice was carried on by his successor, Emilio del Cavalieri.

In this way the word oratorio came into general use.

Later, performances of oratorio were given in concert halls, as well as in churches.

You will find that many of the great composers have written oratorios: Bach, Handel, Haydn, Mendelssohn, etc. In 1931 the English composer, Sir William Walton, composed a fine oratorio called 'Belshazzar's Feast'. The style of this music is very different from that of Handel and Mendelssohn, but the story is based on incidents from the Bible.

(b) OPERA

Oratorio and opera both sprang from the same root. In fact, opera is a newer branch of the same tree.

A colourful framework has been given to opera by the use of stage settings, costumes and acting. As the centuries moved forward, religious subjects were gradually replaced by classical stories (myths of Greece and suchlike), and about 1600 an Italian composer named JACOPO PERI wrote his 'Euridice'. This is considered to be the first opera as we know it today.

'Euridice' was sung and acted to the accompaniment of about ten instruments, which were placed behind the scenes.

This new form became popular with the public, and in time other stories, even comic subjects, were presented in operatic form.

MONTEVERDI (1567–1643) still further advanced opera and from then on we find important names coupled with this art: names such as LULLY (1639–87), ALESSANDRO SCARLATTI (1659–1725), PURCELL (1658–95), HANDEL (1685–1759), PERGOLESI (1710–36), GLUCK (1714–87), MOZART (1756–91), BEETHOVEN (1770–1827), who wrote only one opera, WEBER (1786–1826), MEYERBEER (1791–1864), ROSSINI (1792–1868), VERDI (1813–1901), WAGNER (1813–83) and PUCCINI (1858–1924).

These are only the chief names linked with opera.

Opera, like every other form of music, continued to progress. Gradually kings and princes took the place of gods on the operatic stage until the time came when composers used stories about ordinary, everyday people. In 1910 Puccini brought out a new opera called 'The Girl of the Golden West', the story being set in a mining camp in California during the gold rush of 1849–50.

And composers are still writing operas: to name only two, BENJAMIN BRITTEN and GIAN CARLO-MENOTTI.

(c) THE SONATA

During the 17th century composers wrote sets of pieces in dance forms for harpsichord, clavichord, violin or flute and called them suites. These suites were divided into sections, or movements, each in contrast to the other. One would be jolly, another sad, one broad and stately, another light and graceful.

Out of the suite grew the SONATA, the word meaning a piece of music to be sounded (on an instrument), in contrast to a piece to be sung. Instead of a set of varied dance tunes (unrelated pieces) in the suite, the sonata became a composition in which all three (or four) movements arose out of the themes announced near the beginning of the work.

We could, in broad terms, compare a three-movement sonata to a three-act play.

After the curtain rises the actors give us an idea what the play is about.

They give us the main theme. Then another character, or set of characters, may introduce another subject, or a second story in the plot. This would be like the first and second subjects of a sonata.

The second act may wander a little from the main plot, but in the third act matters straighten out, and by the time the final curtain comes down everything has been tied up and rounded off.

A sonata moves along similar lines. In the first movement the composer lets us hear the principal subject (or theme) and, a little later, the second subject. The second movement is often much slower than the others and in it different musical ideas (like characters or situations in a play) appear. All this gives contrast. In the third movement the original subject reappears, mixes with the other musical 'characters', and the whole sonata is tied up and rounded off.

We should remember, however, that a sonata is usually written for one or two instruments. Thus we speak of sonata for violin, sonata for piano, sonata for violin and piano, and so on.

The earliest composers to develop the sonata were HAYDN (1732–1809), MOZART (1756–91) and BEETHOVEN (1770–1827).

(d) THE SYMPHONY

What has been said about the sonata might also be applied, broadly, to the symphony. It is rather like a sonata for orchestra.

Many symphonies take longer to play than sonatas: some lasting from thirty to forty minutes, others for as long as an hour. A symphony is played by the whole orchestra without soloists. There are some, however, in which the composer has written a part for a solo instrument, even a singer, but they are rare. It might also be mentioned that in his Ninth ('Choral') Symphony Beethoven used a full chorus and solo singers towards the end of it. Such cases are not usual.

(e) THE CONCERTO

When the word CONCERTO was first used (in the early 17th century) it meant a composition for orchestra, in which two or three instruments played solo parts with the rest of the orchestra. The concerto later developed into a three (or four) movement work, in which the solo instrument (piano, violin, 'cello, organ, etc.) played his own part against the accompanying full orchestra. Like the symphony, the concerto usually follows the sonata form. That is, it consists of three or four separate parts, known as movements.

Some later composers, for instance Liszt and Delius, wrote one-movement concertos. In these the music, although played without break, varied in mood.

In recent years the word 'concerto' has been loosely applied to short pieces, usually in one movement and lasting less than ten minutes.

Some of these have been written specially for films. Their lack of form and design do not rightly entitle them to be called concertos.

(f) CHAMBER MUSIC

Chamber music was originally intended for use in a room smaller than a concert-hall; in other words, a chamber. Today it is taken to mean a work to be performed by from three to eight players, each having a separate part written for him. Several players might perform the same part; that is, all playing from the same music sheet, but that would not be true chamber music. Each instrument must be treated independently, but all sounding agreeably together.

A string quartet consists of a first violin, a second violin (their parts corresponding to soprano and alto in singing), a viola, and a 'cello. Add a piano or a clarinet to this combination and we have a quintet. A violin, 'cello, and piano would make up a trio.

(g) 'PROGRAMME' MUSIC

Music intended to tell a story, or paint a musical picture, is often referred to as 'programme' music.

Liszt was one of the first composers to write TONE POEMS (or SYMPHONIC POEMS), by which we could follow a story in sound. Saint-Saëns and Richard Strauss (no relation to Johann Strauss, the waltz composer), took up this idea and many later composers have used this interesting form. This is distinct from 'Absolute' music; i.e., a Bach fugue, a Beethoven sonata or a Mozart symphony.

The following are examples of 'programme' music:

Saint-Saëns composed a tone poem entitled 'Danse Macabre', sometimes called 'Dance of Death'. He asked us to imagine a graveyard at night. The piece begins with twelve strokes of the village clock. (The harp plays this.) It is midnight. Death tunes his violin and invites the spirits from their graves to come and dance. A wild orgy follows. We can hear the skeletons (represented by the xylophone) prancing clumsily about. The oboe impersonates the cock crowing at dawn. This is the signal for the spirits to scamper back to their graves.

In the symphonic poem 'Don Quixote' by Richard Strauss, we follow the adventures of that queer knight. In one passage we hear the baa-ing of sheep; in another the groan of a windmill. All are suggested by the instruments in the orchestra.

You probably know 'The Flight of the Bumble Bee' by Rimsky-Korsakov. Hearing this, particularly when played on the violin, we immediately imagine the buzzing of that active little fellow.

In his 'Pastoral' Symphony Beethoven paints a musical picture of a party of merrymakers in a woodland glen; a scene by a brook; the song of birds, and a storm, the work ending with a hymn of thanksgiving because the storm has passed. Beethoven suggested these pictures by clever writing for various instruments.

Yes, the composer creates pictures in sound to be appreciated through the ear just as the artist makes pictures to be appreciated through the eye. In music of the suggestive ('impressionistic') kind we *see through the ear*, as it were.

In Chapter 3 reference was made to 'Music of Machines' and 'Pacific 231'. These are two examples of music which can suggest a picture without actually telling a story.

The above are merely a few of the many examples of 'programme' music.

(h) THE FUGUE

What happens in a fugue is this. The composer announces his subject (or theme) during the first few bars. Then he allows another 'voice' to take it up. Perhaps a third or fourth 'voice' enters with the same tune. These chase each other through the whole composition, sometimes slipping into other keys.

A good way to learn how a fugue is built is to listen carefully to one being played. You will notice how the parts enter and fall out again in a merry 'catch-me-if-you-can' kind of way. This explains the word 'fugue', which comes from the Latin, meaning 'flight'.

The greatest writer of fugues was Johann Sebastian Bach.

SUGGESTED RECORDS

ORATORIO
    MESSIAH, solo: 'Comfort Ye and Every Valley'; chorus: 'And the Glory' (*Handel*)
OPERA
    ORFEO ED EURIDICE, solo: 'What is Life?' (Che faro?) (*Gluck*)
    RIGOLETTO, solo: 'Questa o Quello' (*Verdi*)
    FLYING DUTCHMAN, Spinning Chorus and Sailors' Chorus (*Wagner*)
SONATA
    SONATA No. 5 IN F MAJOR, Op. 24, 'Spring' (*Beethoven*)
SYMPHONY
    SYMPHONY No. 6 IN F MAJOR, 'Pastoral' (*Beethoven*)
    SIMPLE SYMPHONY (*Britten*)
CONCERTO
    BRANDENBURG CONCERTO No. 3 (*Bach*)
    TRUMPET CONCERTO IN E FLAT MAJOR (*Haydn*)
CHAMBER MUSIC
    CANZONETTA FROM QUARTET No. 1 IN E FLAT MAJOR, Op. 12 (*Mendelssohn*)
    TRIO No. 7 IN B FLAT, Op. 97, 'Archduke' (*Beethoven*)
'PROGRAMME' MUSIC
    DANSE MACABRE (*Saint-Saëns*)
    THE SORCERER'S APPRENTICE (*Dukas*)
    THE CARNIVAL OF THE ANIMALS (*Saint-Saëns*)
    PACIFIC 231 (*Honegger*)
FUGUE
    'LITTLE' FUGUE IN G MINOR (*Bach*)

8

Opus numbers and musical terms

In case you are one of the many who wonder what 'op' means when placed after the title of a musical work, we'll clear up this matter at once.

A composer may have written two or more works in the same form (symphonies, concertos, or sonatas) and in the same key. To avoid confusion, he added another label to the title—OPUS, often printed as OP. (For instance, Beethoven composed two symphonies in the key of F major. One is Op. 68, the other Op. 93.)

Opus is the Latin word for 'work', meaning in this case a composition. This system came into use in the 17th century to give numbers to the works of an individual composer. So an opus number serves the same purpose as an index number for the works of each composer.

In some cases several works of the same kind may be included in one opus number: e.g., Beethoven's set of six string quartets are all grouped under Opus 18.

You may have noticed the letter 'K' after the title of a work by Mozart. This composer wrote so many works (over six hundred) during his short life of thirty-five years, that something had to be done about indexing them for easy reference. A botanist named KOCHEL took up the task and, starting from Mozart's earliest composition, he classified them all and gave each a number. When you see the letter 'K' after the title of a work by Mozart, such as K.315, you will know that it means number 315 in the Kochel list. Sometimes this is written 'K.V.', standing for KOCHEL VERZEICHNIS, meaning Kockel list.

MUSICAL TERMS

The following musical terms, indicating pace, force and style, are some of the more frequently used. The examples given are Italian words, as this is the language most generally used.

Pace

Grave	very slow
Adagio	slow, broad, leisurely

Largo	slow, solemn
Larghetto	rather slow
Lento	lingering, less slow than *Largo*
Andante	literal meaning 'going'. Moving easily
Andantino	not so easy-going as *Andante*
Moderato	moderate
Allegro	lively, brisk
Allegretto	less lively than *Allegro*
Presto	fast
Prestissimo	very fast

Alteration to pace

Accelerando or *accel*	increase the pace
Ad libitum or *ad lib*	at pleasure, at liberty
A tempo	returned to original pace
Rallentando or *rall*	decrease the pace

Degrees of softness, loudness or force

Piano (p)	soft
Mezzo piano (mp)	moderately soft
Pianissimo (pp)	very soft
Forte (f)	loud
Mezzo forte (mf)	moderately loud
Fortissimo (ff)	very loud
Crescendo (cres.)	increasing in loudness
Decrescendo (decres.)	decreasing in loudness
Diminuendo (dim.)	decreasing in loudness
Morendo	dying away
Dolce	sweet, gently

Style

Agitato	agitated
Animato	animated
Appassionato	impassioned
Assai	enough or very
Cantabile	in a singing style
Con	with
Con brio	with spirit
Con espressione	with expression
Con spirito	with lively spirit
Espressivo	in an expressive manner
Legato	smoothly
Maestoso	majestically
Molto	much, very
Troppo	too much (*ma non troppo* = but not too much)
Vivace	lively

c

9

Dancing through the centuries

Dancing is a natural instinct. It belongs to all times and to all peoples. Since primitive days, man has expressed his feelings—joy, anger, hope, etc.—in movement. That is, rhythmical movement. Later this became a succession of movements that evolved as dancing, accompanied by appropriate sound-making.

Dancing in its early stages was based on emotion and was soon used in ritual and ceremonies. From carvings and other records we have evidence that the Egyptians used the dance in religious and secular (worldly) ritual as far back as six thousand years ago. As time went on the Greeks brought dancing to a high standard. But we must remember that dancing goes back to those early days when primitive tribes worked off their feelings in rhythmic movement.

It would need many pages to explain all dance forms, but let us take some of them, more or less at random, that have given us their own particular forms of music.

First, the SARABANDE. This stately dance came from Spain and dates from the 12th century. It was later taken up in France and other countries. Many early composers included a sarabande in their suites.

Next, the GAVOTTE, which originally came from that part of France where the inhabitants were called Gavots. The gavotte was adopted by the Court of Louis the Fourteenth, and became so popular that many great composers like Lully, Bach, Gluck and Handel included a gavotte movement in their suites.

Then we have the gavotte's graceful sister, the MINUET. This dainty measure was also popular at Louis XIV's court and danced its way into many countries.

During the 16th and 17th centuries an English dance called the HORNPIPE also became very popular. Some books tell us that its name came from a pipe made from the horns of animals. Once danced in the theatres by actors between the scenes of a play, the hornpipe became a favourite with sailors. Handel included a merry hornpipe in his 'Water Music'.

Then the WALTZ lilted its charming way into music. It is thought that it made its first appearance towards the close of the 18th century in Germany. Different kinds of waltzes, dainty, gay, sad and even boisterous, have taken their place in music. Chopin, who was half Polish and half French, treated the waltz elegantly. The Viennese waltz (also in 3/4 time) had its most popular composer in Johann Strauss (the younger), who wrote the 'Blue Danube'.

The MAZURKA came from Poland and was originally sung as well as danced. Chopin, who was born in Poland, wrote fifty-six mazurkas, each refined in his own graceful style.

Early in the 19th century the POLKA first set feet twirling to its gay rhythm in Bohemia. Before long it had migrated to other countries.

Dancing is based on rhythm and not merely on time. It has already been said in this book that the waltz and the mazurka are both written in 3/4 time, but their styles and their pulses are quite different.

Dances may be grouped in this way: early ritual, folk, court, art dance (as in the classic Italian ballet), modern ballet, and modern ballroom dance.

SUGGESTED RECORDS

SARABANDE, from French Suite No. 3 (*Bach*), piano
GAVOTTE (*Handel*), guitar
MINUET IN G MINOR (*Handel*), piano
WALTZES (*Chopin*), piano
MAZURKAS (*Chopin*), piano
SUITE No. 4 IN D MAJOR (*Bach*)
POLKA from 'The Bartered Bride' (*Smetana*)
'BLUE DANUBE' and 'EMPEROR' WALTZES (*J. Strauss*)
WALTZES, POLKAS AND MARCHES (*J. Strauss*)

10

To mention a few composers

'It would take many hundreds of pages to give the life-stories of all the great composers, so we will deal briefly with those names one is likely to meet today in concert and radio programmes, and on record labels.

Let us start with the 16th century and work up to the present time.

16TH CENTURY

Palestrina, Giovanni Pierluigi de Palestrina   (1525–94) Italy
This great composer took his name from the place of his birth, the small cathedral town of Palestrina. He became prominent in the development of church music and, by giving it a new dignity, saved it from being expelled from the Catholic service. His 'Missa Papae Marcelli' is one of the finest masses of its kind in existence.

Byrd, William   (1542–1623) England
Byrd is understood to have been born at Lincoln, where he became church organist. As well as introducing the English madrigal school, he became esteemed as the father of British music. Apart from his choral music, he wrote many pieces for the virginal, viol, and organ. The number of his works which have been preserved is in excess of that of any other English composer of that period.

17TH CENTURY

Corelli, Archangelo   (1653–1713) Italy
One of the first great violonist-composers. He advanced violin technique and musical forms, and influenced 17th-century musical thought.

Purcell, Henry   (1658–95) England
Often referred to as 'The Flower of English Composers', Purcell was born, lived and died in London. At twenty-two he was appointed organist at Westminster Abbey. He composed for the church theatre and for ceremonial occasions. His opera, 'Dido and Aeneas', written for a girls' school in London, remains one of the richest treasures of English opera.

18TH CENTURY

Scarlatti, Alessandro   (1659–1725) Italy
This composer was an excellent performer on the organ and harpsichord and amongst his writings were operas, cantatas, oratorios, and sonatas. He created the Italian overture, which broke away from the French style of overture.

Scarlatti, Domenico   (1685–1757) Italy
A son of Alessandro, he advanced harpsichord playing and helped to lay the foundation for keyboard playing of the future. He was a firm friend of Handel.

Handel, George Frederick   (1685–1759) Germany
Handel was born at Halle in Saxony, but wrote his greatest music in London. From the age of five he showed outstanding musical ability. While still a child, his organ playing attracted the attention of an important duke who persuaded Handel senior to allow his talented son to take up music study seriously.

He became one of the finest organists of his day. He later took up court positions as violinist and composer, and, on coming to London, became the leading musical figure there.

Handel wrote in many forms: suites, concertos, opera, organ music and oratorio. His oratorio 'Messiah', first performed in Dublin in 1742, still stands with the greatest of its kind. He was buried in the Poets' Corner in Westminster Abbey.

Bach, Johann Sebastian   (1685–1750) Germany
Although born in the same year as Handel, these two great musicians never actually met, yet on one occasion they stood only a few yards from each other.

As a boy, Bach is said to have copied in secret an entire volume of music by moonlight because his brother forbade him the use of the book. The task took six months. We also read that this determined boy would often walk from his school to Hamburg, a distance of twenty-five miles each way, merely to hear the organ played by a musician named Reinken.

At the age of fifteen he was left to earn his own living and at eighteen secured the position of organist and choirmaster at a new church in Arnstadt, his salary being a little over £8·50 per year.

Bach became a very great organist and composed music for that instrument which has never been excelled. He wrote for other instruments and the orchestra of his time. His church music included over two hundred cantatas. Only one of these cantatas was published in his lifetime. The rest of them remained in manuscript, and were sold in bundles after his death for a few pence each.

His Mass in B minor and the Passions (according to St John and St Matthew) are great monuments in choral music.

During Bach's last years his eyesight failed him. Finally he lost it altogether. In 1750 he died peacefully, leaving several of his sons to follow the path of music.

After his death a great many of his works remained neglected until discovered by Mendelssohn (1809–47), who brought them to the notice of the musical world.

Gluck, Christoph Willibald (1714–87) Germany

Born at Weidenvang on the border of Bohemia, Gluck studied in Vienna and Italy and reformed opera by ridding it of cheap, artificial practices. He was perhaps the first composer to lay down the theories that the music, poetry, and dramatic situations should be moulded in such a way to give reality in opera; that the singers should have music fitted to the story and not merely solos that showed off their voices; that simplicity and dignity should replace disconnected vocal gymnastics.

In short, Gluck gave opera a spring-cleaning and laid down the theory that its music was the servant of the drama, and not just a medium for vain singers.

Haydn, Franz Joseph (1732–1908) Austria

The son of a poor wheelwright, Haydn taught himself to play the harp and, as a very young child, amused himself imitating violinists he had heard by scraping one piece of wood across another. Early in life he was appointed musical director to Prince Esterhazy, a position he held for thirty years.

Although it cannot be said that he invented the symphony, he gave it new life and importance and composed more than a hundred of them.

Among his other works are forty-two piano sonatas, eighty-three string quartets, thirty-five trios, and the oratorios 'The Seasons' and 'The Creation'.

Haydn possessed a happy nature and this is often reflected in his music. One day he bought some toy instruments at a village fair. When he reached home he wrote his 'Toy' Symphony, using in its score six of these, including a child's drum, a cuckoo, a quail and a toy nightingale.

He was fond of practical jokes in music, and this can be noticed in his 'Joke' Quartet, and his 'Farewell' and 'Surprise' Symphonies.

Not long before his death a war broke out, and a mile from his house French shells battered his beloved Vienna. Four shells fell close by, and some of his servants fled in terror. He asked those who remained to carry him to his piano. There he played, and, in a feeble voice, sang 'God Preserve the Empire'.

Mozart, Wolfgang Amadeus (1756–91) Austria

By the age of seven Mozart was a brilliant performer on the clavier and the violin, and had already composed many pieces. A manuscript of a minuet which he wrote down at the age of five is still preserved.

While still a young child, accompanied by his sister, he was taken on a concert tour by his father. Soon Vienna, Prague, and London honoured him as a young genius.

The outstanding quality of Mozart's music was the result of his attention to detail. Although he lived only thirty-five years, he left over six hundred compositions, including forty-one symphonies, a great number of concertos, orchestral pieces, sonatas and string quartets, and several truly great operas, including 'Don Giovanni', 'The Marriage of Figaro', 'The Magic Flute' and 'Il Seraglio'.

He was buried in a pauper's grave in Vienna, the place of which is unknown today.

Beethoven, Lugwig van   (1770–1827) Germany

Beethoven is one of the greatest composers the world has ever known. Even during his lifetime he was recognised as a powerful figure in music.

He was born at Bonn, on the Thine, at the time the boy Mozart was bringing in good money to his parents. Ludwig's father, who liked money better than anything else, wanted his own son to be a wonder-child like Wolfgang Mozart, and kept him at the piano day and night.

Beethoven became a really fine pianist, and when he began to compose, both Mozart and Haydn foretold a brilliant future for him. At the age of thirty-two his hearing was so poor that he was forced to give up playing and so he settled down to composition for the rest of his life.

He loved nature and did much of his composing in the woods, jotting down his ideas in a notebook. His love for the country is beautifully expressed in his 'Pastoral' (6th) Symphony.

Over twenty-five thousand people followed his funeral in Vienna, including Franz Schubert, who, the next year, was laid to rest beside him.

Beethoven's works include nine symphonies, five piano concertos and one violin concerto, seventeen quartets, two quintets, thirty-two sonatas for piano, ten sonatas for violin and piano, *missa solemnis*, songs, and the opera 'Fidelio', as well as other orchestral, chamber and piano music.

Weber, Carl Maria von   (1786–1826) Germany

Weber's chief importance lies in German romantic opera, of which he was the founder.

He was born at Eutin in Lower Saxony, the son of a musician. As a child he made only slow progress in the study of the violin. Later he was taken as a pupil by Michael Haydn, a brother of the famous composer, Franz Joseph.

He became famous as a writer of operas, was appointed director of the opera house at Breslau, and later music master to the King of Saxony.

He wrote sonatas, concertos, and other kinds of music, but he is best known for his operas 'Der Freischutz', 'Oberon', and 'Euryanthe'.

Schubert, Franz   (1797–1828) Austria
Schubert's greatness rests to a large extent on his songs. He wrote six hundred of them.

He was poor and unrecognised in his own time and his life was not always happy, but melody flowed from his pen. By the time he was eighteen he had written more music than many composers manage in a lifetime. In his short life of thirty-one years he composed more than a thousand works, these in most forms, yet in the winding-up of his estate a bundle of his manuscripts was valued at about 40p.

19TH CENTURY

Mendelssohn, Felix Mendelssohn-Bartholdy   (1809–47) Germany
With Mendelssohn we enter into the 'classical-romantic' era, for he wrote polished music in the 'classic' style, but often chose romantic subjects and a romantic way of expressing them.

Unlike many great composers of the past, Mendelssohn never knew poverty. He had a happy life, surrounded by love, comfort, and even luxury. His father was a wealthy banker in Hamburg. From his mother he had his first music lessons, and while still in his 'teens was an excellent pianist and organist, and also recognised as a promising composer. Among his close friends were Schumann and Chopin.

Mendelssohn's music is notable for its perfection of detail, not always profound, but rich in melody.

At the age of seventeen, he composed his 'Midsummer Night's Dream' Overture, which is considered one of his best works.

He travelled a good deal and visited Italy and England several times, his greatest oratorio 'Elijah' having its first performance in Birmingham.

His Concerto in E Minor, Op. 64, is included among the best violin concertos.

Schumann, Robert   (1810–56) Germany
Born a year later than Mendelssohn, Schumann is often referred to as the 'Founder of the Romantic Movement in Music'.

His birthplace was Saxony, not far from where Handel was born. He appears to have been an ordinary boy, good at games, and conspicuous in any sport or adventures his young friends had in hand.

By using a contrivance he had invented for strengthening his fingers, he crippled his hand for life. He turned to composition, and the world lost a pianist, but gained a composer.

He had studied with a teacher named Wieck, whose daughter he married. She was a brilliant pianist and played his piano music in various parts of the world.

In 1854 he suffered a mental illness and died two years later in a private asylum.

His best writing is to be found in his piano works and songs. During the first year of his married life he composed over a hundred songs, as well as other important music. His works include symphonies and chamber music.

Chopin, Frederic (1810–49) Poland

Chopin is probably the best-known composer of music for the piano. Indeed, apart from some songs and some other pieces, he wrote almost exclusively for piano. His works include two concertos for piano and orchestra, three sonatas, fifty-six mazurkas, nineteen nocturnes, four ballades, as well as preludes, waltzes, études (studies), scherzos, etc.

He was half French and half Polish. He spent part of his life in his native Poland, the remainder in France, and so we find in his music the sadness of one country and the grace and elegance of the other.

He began his career as pianist at nine, but studied hard for many years after. The homes of the aristocracy were always open to him.

Taking leave of his native Warsaw at the age of twenty-one, he took with him a silver casket containing some earth of his beloved country. In 1849 this was scattered over his coffin. His heart was sent back to Warsaw, where it lay in peace in a church for close on a century, until 1939 when German bombs destroyed the building.

Berlioz, Hector (1803–69) France

The chief importance of Berlioz lay in his gift for orchestration. He knew the full possibilities of every instrument, gave each a new scope and introduced new effects in orchestral writing.

The son of a prominent doctor, Berlioz struck out a career for himself, grew up rather quarrelsome and eccentric, but his musicianship and scholarly attainments were never questioned.

His best-known works are: 'Fantastic' Symphony, 'Childhood of Christ', 'Damnation of Faust', 'Romeo and Juliet', 'Corsair' and 'Carnival Romain' Overtures.

Liszt, Franz (1811–86) Hungary

Probably the greatest pianist the world had ever known, Liszt devoted much effort to making known the music of neglected composers, and did a great deal to advance the reputation of Brahms, Schumann, Wagner, and others.

His Hungarian rhapsodies, concertos, tone poems and piano pieces are frequently performed, also his transcriptions for piano of some songs by Schubert and Schumann.

In later life he became an Abbé.

Wagner, Richard (1813–83) Germany

Wagner was one of the most colourful figures in 19th-century music.

He spent much of his boyhood with his stepfather, an actor, and so learned a great deal about stagecraft. Like Gluck, a century before him,

Wagner tired of cheap effects and tawdry frills that had again crept into opera and, with a deep respect for dramatic truth, created what became known as the 'music-drama'.

For his material he chose age-old legends. He even introduced dragons, gods and spectacular stage effects in his productions. Because his music-dramas call for a large space, these are not often produced outside the largest theatres.

To gain realism he broke many old laws, but he knew what he wanted. Many of his orchestral scores call for a hundred players, many of whom at first found some of his music almost too difficult to perform.

His greatest music-dramas are: 'The Ring', a series of four operas entitled 'The Rhinegold', 'The Valkyries', 'Siegfried', and 'Twilight of the Gods'; also 'Tannhäuser', 'Lohengrin', 'Parsifal' and 'Tristan and Isolde'. He also wrote a lighter opera entitled 'The Mastersingers of Nuremburg'.

(Have you noticed how many great composers were born at the beginning of the 19th century?)

Franck, César   (1822–90) Belgium

Although born in Belgium, César Franck studied and lived in Paris and became a very important figure in French music.

As a young student, he sat for an examination and was given two short themes and asked to improvise on them. That is to say, he was required to build a larger composition on the themes, each in turn. He saw how these could be combined. So he played them together, with great skill and at considerable length.

The examiners were so bewildered that they decided not to pass him at all! His teacher pleaded for him and he was afterwards awarded second prize. You see, Franck was another composer who was ahead of his time.

He became a successful organist and teacher, and his gentle nature endeared him to everyone.

Among his works are those for organ, piano and orchestra.

Brahms, Johannes   (1833–97) Germany

Brahms was a further link between the classical and romantic periods in music. He was born early in the romantic era, but clung to a classical style and combined the two. It was as though he was born after his time.

He took up the composing of song where Schubert left off, and the symphony from Beethoven.

At school Brahms' progress was not encouraging, but at fifteen he was a capable pianist. As a young man he wrote much music which he later destroyed. He was a hard critic of his own work, and waited until he has mastered his art before giving his music to the world.

Like Beethoven, Mendelssohn and Tchaikovsky, Brahms composed only one violin concerto, but it is one of the greatest ever written. His other works are: four symphonies, two concertos for piano, chamber, piano and orchestral music, songs and choral works, 'A German Requiem' (in memory of his mother) and 'Song of Destiny'.

Saint-Saëns, Camille   (1835–1921) France

Someone once spoke of this French composer as 'the greatest musician who was not a genius'.

He began composing at the age of seven, and during his long life wrote in almost every musical form.

Among his best-known works are the tone poem 'Danse Macabre', 'Carnival of the Animals', piano concertos and the opera 'Samson and Delilah'.

Tchaikovsky, Peter Ilyich   (1840–93) Russia

One of the most universally loved composers, Tchaikovsky did not show any outstanding musical promise as a boy, but later developed a keenness for the piano.

He threw up his job as a clerk and faced a life of poverty for the sake of music. The world owes much to Nedeschda von Meck, a wealthy widow, who settled upon the young composer a yearly income of six thousand roubles so he could devote his whole time to composition. This was on condition that he would at no time make any effort to meet her.

He wrote colourfully for orchestra, completing six symphonies. His other works include one violin concerto, three piano concertos, operas, chamber music, songs and piano pieces.

Dvorak, Antonin   (1841–1904) Bohemia

One of the most gifted of the 19th-century composers, Dvorak was born near Prague of simple peasant stock, his father being the proprietor of a butcher's shop in a small village.

His early compositions show the influence of Mozart and Beethoven, some later works that of Brahms, but in time he developed a style very much his own and became a highly skilful orchestral composer.

His 'New World' Symphony and Slavonic dances are popular the world over.

Grieg, Edvard   (1843–1907) Norway

Grieg was born in Norway, made use of Norwegian and Swedish folk tunes in his compositions, and is regarded as the finest composer of his country.

Most of his works, which are full of melody and charm, are on a small scale, such as piano pieces, songs and incidental music for plays. Among his most famous works are the Concerto in A Minor for piano and orchestra and two 'Peer Gynt' Suites for orchestra.

Rimsky-Korsakov, Nicholas (1844–1908) Russia

Rimsky-Korsakov served for six years in the Navy, but spent his spare time on Sundays and holidays mastering the 'cello and piano. He became a composer of outstanding quality, and was later appointed professor of music at the St Petersburg Conservatorium.

His works are vividly colourful, often exciting, and of superb craftsmanship. Among the best-known are 'Scheherazade', 'Le Coq d'or', 'Sadko' and 'Capriccio Espagnol'.

Elgar, Sir Edward (1857–1934) England

For some time English music had failed to advance. Then Elgar appeared on the scene and certain authorities found in him the greatest English composer since Purcell.

As a boy Elgar picked up a good deal of knowledge in his father's music shop. Some violin lessons were the only other training in music that he ever received. He taught himself to play the organ and also conducted a band at the county mental asylum. The latter gave him a knowledge of instruments that was to prove valuable to him.

Elgar composed in three styles. His early works were pretty little pieces. Then, as Master of the King's Musick, he wrote stirring marches, such as 'Pomp and Circumstance'. His oratorio 'Dream of Gerontius', 'The Apostles', violin concerto and symphonies have placed his name among the great. He wrote in a broad, rather 'modern' manner, but built on the same foundation Beethoven had used.

He was knighted in 1904 by King Edward VII.

Debussy, Claude (1862–1918) France

We know little about Debussy as a child, apart from the fact that he collected butterflies and wanted to be a painter. This may have meant something, because he used colour in music perhaps more than any other composer before him.

He was a very good pianist. At the Conservatoire he carried off first prize for accompanying on the piano, but in composition was told he had made six mistakes in twenty-seven bars. The truth was he was thinking ahead of his time and inventing a new form of writing. He had an original mind and saw new possibilities for piano tone-colour.

As a young man he was poor. In fact, on the morning of his wedding day he had to give a piano lesson to pay for the day's expenses.

In much of Debussy's music there is the sound of water. For him the sea was a mighty force, full of its own thoughts. About 1887 he founded what is known as the *'Impressionist'* school, the word 'impressionism' being borrowed from painting, meaning that by an arrangement of sounds—or harmonies—the composer can give us a mental picture, or an impression.

Today Debussy is considered one of the best composers of the modern French school. His writing included many piano pieces, songs, much chamber music, and such orchestral works as 'Iberia', 'La Mer' 'L'aprè-midi d'un faune', and the opera 'Pelléas et Mélisande'.

Delius, Frederick   (1862–1934) England

As you will see, Delius was born in the same year as Debussy and died in the same year as Elgar.

He was the son of a German-born merchant who became a naturalised Englishman. As a young man, Frederick lived on an orange plantation in Florida. He accepted the Norwegian Grieg as a model, studied in Germany, but spent most of his life in France.

Much of his music has a misty, poetic quality. There is no doubt he created a style of writing completely his own.

Among his best-known works are: 'On Hearing the First Cuckoo in Spring', 'Brigg Fair', 'Summer Night on the River', 'A Village Romeo and Juliet', violin sonatas, violin and piano concertos, songs, and incidental music to James Elroy Flecker's play 'Hassan'.

Sibelius, Jan   (1865–1957) Finland

Now regarded as one of the greatest composers, Sibelius lost his parents while he was a young child and was brought up by his grandmother. At the age of fifteen he began the study of the violin, hoping to become a great artist. Realising his late start, he taught himself theory, and at twenty he gave up his law studies to devote his time to composition.

Sibelius became so honoured in his own country that the Finnish government arranged for him to give his attention to music without having to bother about money matters.

Among his finest work are his symphonies, Concerto in D Minor for violin and orchestra, symphonic poems (many of which are based on legends of Finland), choral works and some of his hundred songs.

20TH CENTURY

Vaughan Williams, Dr Ralph   (1872–1958) England

This famous musician took the degree of Bachelor of Music at Cambridge while still very young. After studying with Parry and Stanford in England, he became a pupil of Max Bruch in Germany, and later (in Paris) was Ravel's only pupil.

Early in his career he found a keen interest in English folk music, and so we find many of his works based on old English melodies. In addition to symphonies, Vaughan Williams has written choral and orchestral works, a mass, songs, and much other music.

Rachmaninoff, Sergei   (1875–1943) Russia

Rachmaninoff first gained world-wide fame through his Prelude in C Sharp Minor (one of twenty-four) for piano. He was one of the greatest pianists of his time and a very competent conductor.

He was a composer with a great depth of feeling, his works containing a sweet sadness and a beauty of tone-colour that are very moving. Some of his music resembles that of Tchaikovsky.

His compositions include three symphonies, four concertos for piano and orchestra, the splendid 'Rhapsody on a Theme by Paganini', a tone poem, 'Isle of the Dead', numerous piano pieces, songs, etc.

Stravinsky, Igor (b. 1882) Russia

This composer, who gave up his Russian nationality many years ago, studied with Rimsky-Korsakov. After his first symphony appeared in the famous ballet producer Diaghilev asked him to prepare some music for one of his productions. This led to the creation of such ballet works as 'The Firebird', 'Petrouschka' and 'The Rite of Spring'. These had a strong influence on music generally and on ballet particularly.

Some years later he changed his style of writing to a simpler form and produced concertos, 'Symphony of Psalms' (choral), 'Oedipus Rex' (opera-oratorio) and works for piano and orchestra. He has also experimented in the jazz idiom.

Bartok, Bela (1881–1945) Hungary

Although much of Bartok's music may not appeal at first hearing, he must be included with the great modernists. Early this century he became interested in the folk music of Hungary and collected thousands of tunes belonging to the people of that country. On these he based his compositions.

Prokofieff, Serge (1891–1953) Russia

This interesting composer was once a pupil of Rimsky-Korsakov and, like Rachmaninoff, began his career as a brilliant pianist. During his busy life he lived in America and Paris, as well as in his native Russia.

His earlier compositions were strongly criticised as being too extreme in style, but in time his originality and skill were fully recognised. Towards the end of his life he adopted a simpler form of musical expressionism.

Among his chief works are: concertos for piano and violin, symphonies, sonatas, an opera, 'Love for Three Oranges', ballet music, chamber music, 'Lieutenant Kiji' Suite, incidental music for the Russian film 'Alexander Nevsky' and 'Peter and the Wolf'.

Walton, Sir William (b. 1902) England

Born in Lancashire, Walton won praise for his Piano Quartet in 1919. In 1925 his 'Façade' Suite gained him wider fame. During World War II he served with the British Army.

Such works as 'Belshazzar's Feast', his orchestral music and concertos have placed him among the important composers of this century. He wrote the incidental music for the films 'Henry V' and 'Hamlet'.

Shostakovich, Dmitri   (b. 1906) Russia

Shostakovich began composing at the age of thirteen. His First Symphony, carrying hints of Tchaikovsky and Prokofieff, was completed before he was twenty. He is now regarded as one of the most important of present-day Soviet composers.

His works, which contain strong contrasts of wry humour, sad reflection and bounding vitality, include symphonies, concertos, ballet music, chamber music, and an opera, 'The Lady Macbeth of Mstensk'.

Barber, Samuel   (b. 1910) America

Barber was born in Pennsylvania, took up music study at the age of thirteen, and began composing at twenty-two. While still in his twenties he won the Prix de Rome and the Pulitzer Prize for music. His 'Symphony in One Movement' was the first work by an American composer ever to be played at the famous Salzburg Festival.

Two of his most popular orchestral pieces are 'Adagio for Strings' and 'Essay for Orchestra'.

Britten, Benjamin   (b. 1913) England

This brilliant musician was born in Suffolk, studied with John Ireland and the Australian-born Arthur Benjamin, and after leaving the Royal College of Music adopted a style all of his own.

He has written chamber, orchestral and choral music, songs and several operas, the complete list being quite a long one.

11
The lighter side of music

The most famous musicians have shown us that music has a lighter side. Even great composers who have written noble oratorios and symphonies have seen the funny side of things and have introduced humour into the world of sound we know as music.

Take Haydn, for instance. This beloved composer wrote works which have been called 'sublime', 'noble' and 'tender'. But he was a genial, good-humoured man, and these personal qualities found their way into his music.

Now, Haydn had noticed that during quiet music the ladies in the court audience would often drop off to sleep. Perhaps they had eaten too much. So, in his 'Surprise' Symphony he included a movement in which a very quiet passage was suddenly interrupted by a crashing chord.

'That should make the ladies jump', chuckled Haydn.

It did.

A tactful hint

There is another story concerning the same composer.

While engaged by Prince Esterhazy as conductor of the court orchestra, Haydn had repeatedly asked the prince for leave of absence for his musicians and himself. When this overdue holiday was postponed indefinitely, he wrote his 'Farewell' Symphony and had it performed before the prince and his friends.

He had so written the last movement that, one by one, the players stopped, picked up their instruments, blew out the candles on their desks, and walked quietly from the room. Only two violinists were left to play the final bars.

The prince laughed and took the hint. The musicians gained their leave of absence in time for Christmas.

A musical joke

One of Haydn's string quartets (E Flat Major, Opus 33, No. 2) has been nicknamed the 'Joke' Quartet because of the humorous twists the composer has given to the last movement. The best part of the joke is at the very end. Instead of the music completing itself on a final chord, it just reaches an upward tilt and remains there. We wait for the end, but it never comes.

Pity the accompanist
Many a singer has blamed his accompanist for his own mistakes.

A fashionable, but not very good, singer once declared that if Handel did not accompany him better he would jump into the harpsichord.

Handel merely replied: 'Let me know when you intend to do it and I will advertise it. I'm sure more people will come to see you jump than to hear you sing.'

A novel instrument
Gluck was a very serious composer and enjoyed the privileges of court life. But he was not above bringing humour into his musical world. According to a writer of his day, he once 'played a concerto on twenty-six drinking glasses tuned with spring water, accompanied by the whole band, being a new instrument of his own invention; upon which he performs whatever may be done on a violin or harpsichord'.

Fun on the stage
Many opera singers are highly strung, but sometimes their sense of fun gets the better of them. During a performance of Beethoven's sombre opera 'Fidelio' many years ago, the leading soprano (Madame Devrient) had to hand the tenor a crust of bread. As he was slow in taking it, Madame Devrient impatiently asked in a whisper that reached half the audience: 'Why the dickens don't you take it? Do you want it buttered?'

There is a more up-to-date story told about Lotte Lehmann and Richard Tauber, who were appearing together in Weber's opera 'Der Freischutz'. Before the performance one evening Lehmann reminded Tauber that he still owed a bet he had lost—a bar of chocolate.

'You'll get it when you least expect it,' answered the tenor.

During the second act Lehmann stretched out her hand towards her stage lover. Into it Tauber placed an already melting chocolate bar which measured about a foot long. This was later disposed of by dropping it on to a seat, an unfortunate place to have put it, as the villain of the opera, attired in white satin, sat on it and spent the rest of the evening trying to keep his back from the view of the audience.

A Cardinal corrected
Corelli, one of the great violinists of the 17th century, was playing before a select gathering at the house of Cardinal Ottoboni. As the Cardinal's conversation with a guest grew louder, Corelli stopped in the middle of a sonata, laid down his instrument, and politely remarked: 'I fear my music interrupts your grace's conversation.'

D

A discouraging remark

Even kings did not escape the tongues of impatient musicians.

Salomon, a famous London violinist, had for his pupil King George III. During one lesson, when the king's performance was well below standard, his teacher said: 'Violinists, Your Majesty, may be divided into three classes. The first, those who cannot play at all. The second, those who play badly. The third, those who play well. You, sire, have now reached the second class.'

A Monarch insulted

Weber was once unfortunate enough to annoy a certain king who treated him in an offensive manner. One day Weber met an old woman in the palace near the door of His Majesty's room. When she asked where she could find the court washerwoman, the composer, seeing a chance for a little revenge, pointed to the royal door.

'In there,' he said.

The king, who at best of times detested old women, forced the truth from her, and Weber was thrown into prison. He might have remained there for years, had not the king's brother, a close friend of the composer had him released.

A clever ruse

A good story is told about Handel, although there is some doubt about its accuracy.

While engaged as chief musician to George of Brunswick, who afterwards became King George the First of England, Handel paid a visit to London. There he stayed for two years, which, it must be admitted, was quite a long holiday.

When Queen Anne died and Handel's patron ascended the English throne, the composer found himself in ill-favour with the king for deserting his post for such a long time.

Hearing that the king was to take an excursion along the Thames, Handel composed his 'Water Music' and had it performed in a boat following the royal barge. His Majesty appreciated the music—and the ruse—to such an extent that he forgave Handel and added an extra £200 per year to his pension.

Sound judgement

Dr Arne, the composer of 'Rule, Britannia', was asked by two conceited singers to decide which was the better artist.

When the second had sung his piece, Arne said: 'You are the worst singer I have ever heard.'

'Then,' said the other, 'I win.'

'No,' answered Arne, scowling darkly, 'you can't sing *at all*.'

A double meaning

A young lady, who had more self-confidence than voice, once sang to Liszt. He stood the ordeal bravely, and when the 'singer' had finished, remained silent.

She smiled at him, saying, 'They tell me I have a lovely voice.'

Liszt smiled back. '*Lovely* is not the word,' he replied.

An unsocial violin

Sarasate, the great Spanish violinist, was only one of many musicians who disliked having to play at private homes where the guests were likely to enjoy their own chatter more than the performance.

When a lady of fashion sent him an invitation to 'take tea at my home next Tuesday afternoon' and put a footnote: 'Do bring your violin along,' Sarasate replied, 'I'm afraid I must come alone. For, you see, my violin doesn't take tea.'

How Berlioz fooled the critics

Some musicians have indulged their sense of humour by fooling those who, without sufficient knowledge for the task, have set themselves up as musical authorities.

Besides being an important composer, Berlioz was a music critic and enjoyed making fun of less worthy critics. When he introduced his 'Flight into Egypt', written in an old style, he put it on the programme as the work of a 17th-century composer named 'Pierre Ducre'.

Next day the critics spoke highly of the work, one declaring it better than Berlioz' own writings, another going so far as to give details concerning the life of this Pierre Ducre. When these 'clever' writers had fully expressed themselves, Berlioz made it public that the composition was his own and that no such person as Ducre had ever existed.

Thoughtless audiences

Musicians of every generation have, at some time or other, smarted under the thoughtless behaviour of audiences. In fact, they still do.

Hans von Bulow, a famous pianist and conductor of the last century, was noted for his biting wit and for his manner of dealing with members of the audience who annoyed him.

One day, while he was rehearsing an orchestra, several ladies entered the hall and continued to talk loudly. Now, Bulow disliked anyone being present at rehearsals, especially ladies who talked. Just as the visitors' chatter had reached its height, Bulow stopped the orchestra and said quietly, 'We will rehearse the bassoon part.'

These instruments had nothing to play until after thirty-two bars, but Bulow unsmilingly beat time from the beginning of the score. After a few stray notes from the bassoons, there came another period of silence, this time lasting for sixty-four bars. By the time Bulow had finished 'conducting' this uninteresting little-music-and-much-silence, the ladies had taken their leave. After that Bulow had little trouble at his rehearsals from intruders.

During the overture to an opera at Covent Garden some years ago, the famous conductor, Sir Thomas Beecham, silenced some chatterers with a very loud 'Shut up!' Rather harsh, perhaps, but it helped to teach audiences at that opera house good manners during the rest of the season.

In Brisbane Town Hall in 1940, during the overture to the 'Messiah', Beecham called out to some noisy latecomers, 'Will someone please shut that door. This is a concert hall, not a cabaret.'

Getting his own back

Another conductor, Basil Cameron, once created a stir at Harrogate when he conducted a work during which his orchestral players chattered loudly, coughed, sneezed and turned the pages of newspapers, a rebuke to those whose manners in that concert hall had so often irritated him.

Greedy audiences

An artist naturally welcomes enthusiasm from his audience, but at the end of a long, tiring programme, he is inclined to feel annoyed when he is called upon to play encore after encore.

On one occasion when Hans von Bulow had played a difficult programme, followed by several encores, the applause grew more persistent. Coming on to the platform for what he hoped would be the last time that night, he said, 'If you people do not stop this applause, I will play all of Bach's forty-eight preludes and fugues from beginning to end!'

At one of his Melbourne recitals in 1935, the violinist Yehudi Menuhin added eight encores to an exacting programme. When his audience demanded more, Yehudi returned to play his final solo in an overcoat, a polite but definite hint that they had had their money's worth.

They sounded like geese

Remember the story about the geese that saved Rome?

Hans von Bulow was once rehearsing a choir. While he was taking the tenors and basses through their parts, the ladies of the chorus started up a conversation that must have sounded to the conductor like the chatter of geese.

When he could stand it no longer, he called out, 'Ladies, ladies, Rome does not have to be saved tonight.'

It was once thought that musicians lived in a world of their own, a serious world where the sunshine of good humour never entered. This is far from the truth. Besides being ordinary people, many great composers have brought laughter into their works.

Haydn once wrote a composition in which he good-naturedly made fun of an unskilled composer vainly trying to write a symphony. In one of his symphonies Beethoven humorously represents a village band. Chopin's 'Waltz in D Flat, Opus 64, No. 1' became known by the less-dignified title of 'Dog Waltz', because someone said it is supposed to give us a musical picture of a puppy running round and round after his tail.

You've perhaps heard how much fun Saint-Saëns put into his 'Carnival of the Animals' suite. In this, in a good-natured way, Saint-Saëns poked fun at the works of other composers, even his own. For instance, his fellow countryman Berlioz had written a very delicate piece entitled 'Dance of the Sylphs'. These fairy-footed creatures are represented in Saint-Saëns' score by those delightful but ungraceful animals, elephants.

When you hear 'Peter and the Wolf' you will notice how humorously Prokofieff portrays the wolf, the duck, the cat, bird, Peter, and his grandfather, by the clever use of instruments.

These are just a few examples of humour in music. There are many more.

SUGGESTED RECORDS

'SURPRISE' SYMPHONY, No. 94 in G Major (*Haydn*)
'FAREWELL' SYMPHONY, No. 45 in F Sharp Minor (*Haydn*)
'JOKE' QUARTET in E Flat Major, Op. 33, No. 2 (*Haydn*)
EIN MUSIKALISCHER SPASS ('A Musical Jest') in F Major, K.522 (*Mozart*)

12

The history of recorded sound

The story of man's effort to record sound goes back a long way. According to some authorities, it has been traced as far back as four thousand years!

From ancient books it would appear that a Chinese prince possessed a box into which he whispered messages. This he would send to someone in a distant part of the country who, on opening it, would hear clearly the prince's voice and the words he had imprisoned inside it.

Yes, surprising as it may seem to us, China may have discovered some method of recording sound four thousand years ago.

Another writer tells us that about one thousand five hundred years before the Christian era, an Egyptian ruler named Ameoophis had a giant temple erected in Thebes. From one of the large statues, strange harp, or lute-like, sounds issued forth at dawn. Within the statue a contrivance had been placed which mechanically reproduced sound. It was shattered by an earthquake about 27 B.C., and, although restored in A.D. 174, the secret was lost.

There are other references in literature of a past age to 'frozen sounds' and 'congealed voices'.

About 1680 a philosopher named Robert Hooke (who, by the way, saw the possibilities of artificial silk) experimented with the production of sound by means of a toothed wheel revolving against a wooden or metal tongue. About the middle of the 19th century, a French typographer, Leon Scott, recorded sound waves, but did not actually reproduce them.

Towards the end of the 19th century, Faber of Vienna invented a hand-operated mechanism, controlled by a typewriter-like keyboard, and containing a rubber imitation of the human lips and tongue. It also had a device in the throat for rolling 'r's'. About the same time, Kratzenstein produced a machine which pronounced vowel sounds by forcing air through a reed into different hollows or cavities of varying sizes.

Other scientists came forward with many bright ideas, until in 1877 Thomas Alva Edison proved that sound could be reproduced as well as recorded. In the same year Charles Cros had deposited with the Academy of Sciences, France, a description of a machine somewhat similar to that which Edison had brought out, but Edison had already registered the word 'phonograph', a motorless affair which was turned by hand. On this a needle recorded the sound as a series of indentations or grooves on a rotating cylinder covered by tin-foil. When the needle again passed over these grooves, the sound was reproduced.

When the first demonstration was given, the first words people heard were 'Mary had a little lamb', spoken by Edison himself.

It is also interesting to note that, as far back as this, Edison applied for a patent for the *electrical* reproduction of sound, which, however, did not come into force until some years later.

In 1886 Graham Bell (the inventor of the telephone), with an American scientist, Charles Sumner Tainter, brought out the 'graphophone', with a wax record consisting of a cardboard cylinder covered with a mixture of stearine soap, zinc and iron oxides, and a gouge-shaped sapphire cutter. They used separate machines for recording and for reproducing.

Later the cylinder was replaced by the flat disc, and Emile Berliner of Washington changed the system of recording from the up and down ('hill and dale') method to a recording track of even depth, running from side to side. This still applies.

From then on, until 1925, records were made by *acoustic* means. In 1925 *electrical* recording brought a much more faithful quality to the record. This was partly due to two engineers of the Bell Telephone Laboratories, named Maxfield and Harrison.

When using the acoustic method it was necessary for the singer to put his head inside a large horn. His voice was then carried along tubes to the recording unit. The accompanying instruments were placed closely behind him. To allow the instruments to sound louder and clearer, say, between the verses of a song, the singer had to remove his head from the horn to permit more tone to pass through without undue obstruction. For this reason, only a few instruments were used.

Electrical recording allowed a full orchestra to be recorded by correct placing of microphones.

In America, in 1932, the first attempts were made to produce the 'long-playing' record which is so familiar today.

Only gradual progress was made along these lines until 1948, when the long-playing, microgroove record, pressed on vinylite, appeared. This had several advantages over the former 'standard' disc, which was recorded at 78 revolutions per minute. One 12-in. '78' side played for about four to four-and-a-half minutes, which meant that in the case of, say, a symphony, one needed to turn over the records every four minutes or so. The LP record, being recorded at the slower speed of $33\frac{1}{3}$ r.p.m., and having the grooves closer together, plays for upwards of twenty-five to thirty minutes per side. Now we can hear a symphony through without having to change the record.

With the standard 78 record there was a good deal of surface noise. With the microgroove there is almost none.

Through this later method of 'high fidelity' recording we are able to hear qualities of sound which, before, were lost to the ear.

Music-lovers, and music itself, owe a deep debt of gratitude to those skilful people who have brought the gramophone record to its present peak of excellence.

In the late 1950s the 'stereophonic' record came on the market. As the word suggests, stereophonic (shortened to 'stereo') means solid, or three-dimensional, sound. In other words, the stereo record reproduces with added width and depth, and with greater detail, than the 'monaural' (pre-stereo) disc.

Our ears receive stereo sound in much the same way as the two pictures viewed through a stereoscope combine to produce a unified, solid, three-dimensional visual image in true perspective.

In stereo sound our two ears pick up separate left-hand and right-hand details of a performance, and the brain accepts a unified, spread sound.

In the case of monaural recording, the whole performance is picked up by one microphone, and transferred to a single groove on the record. In stereo recording, two (sometimes even three or four) microphones pick up left-hand and right-hand details of the performance, and the sounds from this duplicate (or multiple) microphone system are fed through to the recording apparatus in two separate sound channels, a 'left' channel and a 'right' channel. These two sound channels are conveyed separately to the two walls of the record groove, which may be thought of as resembling the letter 'V'. This means that one wall of the groove records the 'left' channel (with, say, two sections of the orchestra), and the second wall records the 'right' channel (with the other two sections).

Two sound channels have been recorded, and these must now be reproduced.

A special stylus (or diamond) picks up the modulations of the two sound channels from the walls of the groove, and the two simultaneous but distinct series of electrical impulses are amplified and fed to two speakers—one for each channel. These speakers are usually housed in separate cabinets, although sometimes they are placed some distance apart in the one cabinet.

Instead of, say, an orchestra on a stage being funnelled into a single speaker, as in the case of the standard monaural record, the stereo recording is reproduced from two speakers some distance apart, creating the illusion—in fact, the reality—of the width, depth, defnition, and 'colour' of the original performance.

A further advantage of having two-channel stereo equipment installed is that it will not only reproduce stereo records, but will give added reality to monaural records.

Stereophonically recorded performances on tape, instead of discs, are also available from some record companies. These, of course, must be played back through a tape recorder.

13

The importance and care of the gramophone record

Have you ever fully considered the importance of the gramophone record? It is one of the great blessing of this age.

We owe much to Sir Compton Mackenzie who, for over thirty years, has championed this wonderful invention as a force in cultural life. Through his magazine *The Gramophone*, with its information of latest developments and its candid reviews, he has stimulated further interest in the record throughout the English-speaking world. As far back as 1925 he declared: 'The effect of the gramophone record cannot fail to be unimaginably great.'

Since man first imprinted vibrations on a moving surface, the record has progressed from a novelty to a great force in culture and education. By means of the record—in schools, on the radio, and in the home—we can hear the greatest music performed by the greatest artists and orchestras. It can be used to demonstrate the art of good speech. It can preserve for all time the interpretation of great singers and musicians. Our grandchildren will be able to hear how composers of this age played or conducted their own compositions. From their record players, generations yet unborn will be able to hear the oratory of such men as Sir Winston Churchill; or how Bruno Walter rehearsed a Mozart symphony.

Some music is 'beyond us' at first hearing. By playing the record over and over again we become familiar with it and at last realise what the composer intended to convey.

We can listen to an opera or a play in our own homes, knowing that every care has been taken with the performance and the recording of it, for what we hear from the disc is the best the musicians and engineers can give.

The singer need not make a recording on the day his voice is husky; a violinist need not perform if his bow arm is stiff from playing tennis. If the orchestra hasn't given its best, the recording can be done again. If the French horn muffs his entry, just that part can be re-recorded, a piece cut from the tape and the improved piece substituted. You see, the original recording is put on to tape and later transferred to discs.

If you agree that the gramophone record is important and that it is a source of pleasure, then you will realise that every care should be taken to protect it from damage. While it is not easily broken, it is very easily damaged.

To avoid warping, keep it away from heat or cold, even from direct sunlight, and store all your records firmly in an upright position.

Don't leave one on the turntable when not in use, but replace it in its sleeve, handling only the edges, or by an edge and the centre label. Even the natural oil in the skin of a washed thumb will leave its mark.

Before playing, clean the disc with the approved cloth or pad. These are obtainable at record shops. Rubbing with a wrong material or a handkerchief will set up an electrostatic charge and will do more harm than good.

I have seen people who would shudder at the thought of 'dog-earing' pages in a book, treat records so carelessly that my ears have smarted at the result. I wonder how many record dealers have been blamed for selling imperfect records when the damage has been done by the purchaser after he has thoughtlessly mishandled them?

It is amazing how many people expect the stylus (what we used to call the needle) to last forever. If the stylus and the record are treated with care, the stylus will last a good while. If it is asked to track over a scratched surface, it could suffer immediate damage and spoil other discs played by it.

Most record dealers will examine the stylus point for you under a microscope. Don't fail to take advantage of this service. Some experts consider that the diamond point is the most dependable now available.

Small particles of fluff have a habit of settling round the stylus point. Don't try to remove this with the fingers. It should be removed by a very soft artist's brush, camel-hair for preference.

See that your turntable is level: that your record player is not standing on an unven surface. A false level can cause the stylus to sweep across the record and spoil the whole surface. A small spirit gauge will check this.

Remember that the gramophone record is the result of many years of patient research on the part of highly-skilled scientists, engineers and musicians. It is up to you to see that what has gone on to the record comes back to you through the speaker to the best possible advantage.

Select a record dealer you can depend on. Study the record catalogues. Become familiar with the various labels. Keep a watch on dependable record reviews.

The record has much to offer you. Make friends with it.

Remember, also, that we must listen to get the best from music. We can hear without really *listening*. Remember that when good music is being played, remain quiet, if only out of courtesy to the artist, or, in the case of listening to records, the composer.

This book is only an introduction to what can be a very interesting and pleasant study. I can assure you music has much to offer.

Go right ahead and make friends with it.

14
Suggested records for your library

The following list of gramophone records may assist the reader who wishes to move on from those mentioned in previous chapters and build up a record library.

These have been classified under ballet music, concertos, symphonies, etc.

The reader who is only beginning to establish that rewarding friendship with great composers may be advised to start with titles marked *. Others may need more frequent hearing before their true value and appeal are fully appreciated.

Naturally, this list contains only *some* of the countless works that have been recorded. For instance, Schubert composed over six hundred songs, but space allows us to mention only six of them.

Reference can be made to a complete record catalogue obtainable from reliable record dealers, who are also able to offer further advice on what is currently available.

The records suggested are those which are normally in the record catalogue. Because new recorded performances are continually being issued, and many of the older ones being deleted from the catalogue, specific artists and record numbers have not been given.

BALLET MUSIC

*AURORA'S WEDDING (Tchaikovsky)
*BALLET EGYPTIEN (Luigini)
BOLERO (Ravel)
*BOUTIQUE FANTASQUE, LA (Rossini–Respighi)
CARNAVAL (Schumann)
CID, LE (Massenet)
*COPPELIA (Delibes)
*DANCE OF THE HOURS (Ponchielli)
DAPHNIS AND CHLOE (Ravel)
FACADE (Walton)
*'FAUST' BALLET MUSIC (Gounod)
FIREBIRD (Stravinsky)
FRANCESCA DA RIMINI (Tchaikovsky)
GAIETE PARISIENNE (Offenbach)
GAYANEH ('Gayne') (Khatchaturian)
*GISELLE (Adam)

*GOOD HUMOURED LADIES Scarlatti–Tommasini)
JEUX D'ENFANTS (Bizet)
*NUTCRACKER (Tchaikovsky)
*PATINEURS, LES (Meyerbeer–Lambert)
PETROUCHKA (Stravinsky)
*PINEAPPLE POLL (Sullivan–Mackerras)
PULCINELLA (Stravinsky)
RITE OF SPRING (Stravinsky)
*ROSAMUNDE (Schubert)
SCHEHERAZADE (Rimsky-Korsakov)
SEASONS, THE (Glazounov)
*SLEEPING BEAUTY (Tchaikovsky)
*SWAN LAKE (Tchaikovsky)
*SYLVIA (Delibes)
THREE-CORNERED HAT (Falla)
WISE VIRGINS (Bach–Walton)

CHAMBER MUSIC

BEETHOVEN
*STRING TRIOS, Nos. 1, 2 and 3, Op. 9
*PIANO TRIO, in B Flat Major ('Archduke')
PIANO TRIO, No. 5 in D Major, Op. 70 ('Ghost')
*STRING QUARTETS, Op. 18, Nos. 1–6
STRING QUARTETS, Op. 59, Nos. 1, 2 and 3 ('Razumovsky')
STRING QUARTET in C Sharp Minor, Op. 131

BORODIN
STRING QUARTET, No. 2 in D

BRAHMS
*CLARINET QUINTET in B Minor, Op. 115

DVORAK
TRIO in E. Minor, Op. 90 ('Dumky')

HAYDN
*STRING QUARTET No. 5, Op. 3 ('Serenade')
STRING QUARTET, No. 2, Op. 73

MOZART
STRING QUARTETS No. 14 (K.387) and No. 15 (K.421)
*CLARINET QUINTET in A Major (K.515)

SMETANA
STRING QUARTET in E Minor ('From My Life')

SCHUBERT
*PIANO TRIO No. 1 in B Flat Major, Op. 99
*PIANO QUINTET in A Major, Op. 114 ('Trout')
*STRING QUINTET in C Major, Op. 163

SCHUMANN
PIANO QUINTET in E Flat Major, Op. 44

CONCERTOS

Various

BACH, J. S.
*BRANDENBURG, Nos. 1 to 6

Piano

BEETHOVEN
*No. 1 in C Major
*No. 2 in B Flat Major
*No. 3 in C Minor
*No. 4 in G Major
*No. 5 in E Flat Major ('Emperor')

BRAHMS
No. 1 in D Minor
No. 2 in B Flat Major

CHOPIN
*No. 1 in E Minor
*No. 2 in F Minor

GRIEG
*A Minor

LISZT
No. 1 in E Flat Major
No. 2 in A Major

LITOLFF
*Scherzo from Concerto Symphonique

MENDELSSOHN
*No. 1 in G Minor

MOZART
*No. 5 in D Major (K.175)
*No. 15 in B Flat Major (K.450)
No. 21 in C Major (K.467)
No. 24 in C Minor (K.491)
No. 27 in B Flat Major (K.595)

RACHMANINOFF
*No. 2 in C Minor

SAINT-SAËNS
No. 2 in G Minor

SCHUMANN
*A Minor

TCHAIKOVSKY
*No. 1 in B Flat Minor
No. 2 in G Major

Violin

BACH, J. S.
*No. 2 in E Major
D Minor for two violins

BEETHOVEN
*D Major

BRAHMS
*D Major

BRUCH
*G Minor

ELGAR
B Minor

GLAZOUNOV
*A Minor

MENDELSSOHN
*E Minor

MOZART
*No. 4 in D Major (K.218)

PAGANINI
*No. 1 in D Major

SIBELIUS
D Minor

TCHAIKOVSKY
*D Major

VIVALDI
*A Minor for two violins

WIENIAWSKI
No. 2 in D Minor

'Cello

BOCCHERINI
*B Flat Major

DVORAK
*B Minor

HAYDN
*D Minor

SCHUMANN
A Minor

Clarinet

MOZART
*A Major (K.622)

Flute

MOZART
*G Major (K.313)

Oboe

MARCELLO
*C Minor

Organ

HANDEL
*Nos. 1 to 12

Trumpet

HAYDN
*E Flat

OPERA EXCERPTS

(Note: S = Soprano; T = Tenor; M = Mezzo; Bar. = Baritone; B = Bass)

*AFRICANA, L' (*Meyerbeer*)
  O Paradiso (T)
*AÏDA (*Verdi*)
  Celeste Aïda (T)
  Ritorna Vincitor (S)
*BARBER OF SEVILLE (*Rossini*)
  Una voce poco fa (S)
  Ecco ridente in cielo (T)
  Largo al factotum (Bar.)
*BOHÊME, LA (*Puccini*)
  Mia Ciamano Mimi (S)
  Che gelida manina (T)
  Mussetta's Waltz Song (S)
BORIS GODOUNOV (*Moussorgsky*)
  I Have Attained the Highest Power (B)
  Farewell of Boris (B)
*CARMEN (*Bizet*)
  Habanera (S or M)
  Seguidilla (S or M)
  Flower Song (T)
  Toreador Song (Bar.)
*CAVALLERIA RUSTICANA (*Mascagni*)
  Voi lo Sapete (S)
  O Lola (T)
  Intermezzo (Orch.)
*DON GIOVANNI (*Mozart*)
  Vedrai carino (S)
  Batti, batti, o del Masetto (S)
  Il mio tesoro (T)
  Della sua pace (T)
  Madamina (B)
*FAUST (*Gounod*)
  Air de bijou (S)
  Salut! demeure (T)
  Garden Scene (S and T)
  Serenade (B)
  Trio (S, T and B)
  Soldiers' Chorus

FLYING DUTCHMAN (*Wagner*)
  Senta's Ballad (S)
*HANSEL AND GRETEL (*Humperdinck*)
  Sandman's Lullaby (S)
  Evening Prayer (S)
*LOHENGRIN (*Wagner*)
  Elsa's Dream (S)
  Bridal Scene (S and T)
*LUCIA DI LAMMERMOOR (*Donizetti*)
  Mad Scene (S)
  Sextet
*MADAME BUTTERFLY (*Puccini*)
  Un del di (S)
  Love Duet (S and T)
*MAGIC FLUTE (*Mozart*)
  Ach, ich fuhl's (S)
  Tamino's Aria (T)
  O Isis and Osiris (B)
*MANON (*Massenet*)
  The Dream (T)
*MARRIAGE OF FIGARO (*Mozart*)
  Deh vieni (S)
  Porgi amor (S)
  Dove sono (S)
  Porgi amor (S)
  Dove sono (S)
  Non più andrai (Bar.)
*MARTA (*Flotow*)
  M'appari (T)
*TANNHÄUSER (*Wagner*)
  Elisabeth's Greeting (S)
  Elisabeth's Prayer (S)
  O du mein holder Abendstern (Bar.)
  Pilgrims' Chorus
TRISTAN AND ISOLDE (*Wagner*)
  Liebestod (S)
  Love Duet (S and T)

ORATORIO

BELSHAZZAR'S FEAST (*Walton*)
CHILD OF OUR TIMES, A (*Tippett*)
*CREATION, THE (*Haydn*)
DREAM OF GERONTIUS, THE (*Elgar*)

*ELIJAH (*Mendelssohn*)
*MESSIAH (*Handel*)
*SEASONS, THE (*Haydn*)

ORCHESTRAL SUITES

BACH, J. S.
  *SUITE IN D
BIZET
  *ARLESIENNE, L', Nos. 1 and 2
  *FAIR MAID OF PERTH
DEBUSSY
  IMAGES FOR ORCHESTRA
  NOCTURNES FOR ORCHESTRA
ELGAR
  *WAND OF YOUTH
GRIEG
  *HOLBERG
  *LYRIC
  *PEER GYNT, Nos. 1 and 2

HANDEL
  *ROYAL FIREWORKS
  *WATER MUSIC
HOLST
  THE PLANETS
KODALY
  HARY JANOS
MENDELSSOHN
  *A MIDSUMMER NIGHT'S DREAM,
    incidental music
MOUSSORGSKY (*trans. Ravel*)
  *PICTURES AT AN EXHIBITION
SIBELIUS
  KARELIA
TCHAIKOVSKY
  **SUITE No. 1

OVERTURES

ACADEMIC FESTIVAL (*Brahms*)
*BARBER OF SEVILLE (*Rossini*)
*BARTERED BRIDE (*Smetana*)
COCKAIGNE (*Elgar*)
CORIOLAN (*Beethoven*)
*DON GIOVANNI (*Mozart*)
*EGMONT (*Beethoven*)
*1812 (*Tchaikovsky*)
EURYANTHE (*Weber*)
*FINGAL'S CAVE ('Hebrides') (*Mendelssohn*)
*FLEDERMAUS (*J. Strauss*)
FLYING DUTCHMAN (*Wagner*)
*FRA DIAVOLO (*Auber*)
*GYPSY BARON (*J. Strauss*)
LEONORA No. 3 (*Beethoven*)
*LIGHT CAVALRY (*Suppe*)

MAGIC FLUTE (*Mozart*)
*MARRIAGE OF FIGARO (*Mozart*)
MASTERSINGERS, THE (*Wagner*). Prelude
*MERRY WIVES OF WINDSOR (*Nicolai*)
*MIDSUMMER NIGHT'S DREAM (*Mendelssohn*)
OBERON (*Weber*)
*ORPHEUS IN THE UNDERWORLD (*Offenbach*)
*ROMEO AND JULIET (*Tchaikovsky*)
*ROSAMUNDE (*Schubert*)
SCALA DI SETA ('Silken Ladder') (*Rossini*)
*SEMIRAMIDE (*Rossini*)
*TANNHÄUSER (*Wagner*)
*THIEVING MAGPIE (*Rossini*)
TRAGIC (*Brahms*)
*WILLIAM TELL (*Rossini*)
*ZAMPA (*Herold*)

PROGRAMME MUSIC

Orchestral

*DANSE MACABRE (*Saint-Saëns*)
*NIGHT ON A BARE MOUNTAIN (*Moussorgsky*)
*PICTURES AT AN EXHIBITION
   (*Moussorgsky–Ravel*
*MOLDAU ('Ma Vlast') (*Smetana*)
ANTAR (*Rimsky-Korsakov*)
DON JUAN (*R. Strauss*)
DON QUIXOTE (*R. Strauss*)
HERO'S LIFE (*R. Strauss*)

*TILL EULENSPIEGEL (*R. Strauss*)
ACCURSED HUNTER (*César Franck*)
ORPHEUS (*Liszt*)
LES PRELUDES (*Liszt*)
*PEER GYNT (*Grieg*)
LEGENDS FOR ORCHESTRA (*Sibelius*)
*CARNIVAL OF THE ANIMALS (*Saint-Saëns*)
FOUNTAINS OF ROME (*Respighi*)

Piano

*SCENES FROM CHILDHOOD (*Schumann*)
*FANTASIESTÜCKE (*Schumann*)
*CARNAVAL (*Schumann*)

*PICTURES AT AN EXHIBITION (*Moussorgsky*)
CHILDREN'S CORNER SUITE (*Debussy*)
*DANCE OF THE GNOMES (*Liszt*)

SONATAS

Piano

BEETHOVEN
   *Op. 2, No. 3 in C Major
   *Op. 13, No. 8 in C Minor ('Pathetique')
   *Op. 27, No. 14 in C Sharp Minor ('Moonlight')
   *Op. 27 in E Minor
   *Op. 53 in C Major ('Waldstein')
   *Op. 57 in F Minor ('Appassionata')
   No. 106 in B Flat Major ('Hammerklavier')
   Op. 109 in E Major
   Op. 110 in A Flat Major
   Op. 111 in C Minor
BRAHMS
   No. 3 in F Minor, Op. 5

CHOPIN
   *No. 2 in B Flat Minor
   *No. 3 in B Minor
HAYDN
   *No. 35 in C Major
   *No. 37 in D Major
LISZT
   B Minor
MOZART
   *No. 1 in C Major (K.279)
   No. 8 in A Minor (K.31')
   No. 11 in A Major (K.331)
   No. 13 in B Flat Major (K.333)

SCARLATTI
   *E Major (L.23)
   *D Minor (L.43)

Violin and Piano

BACH, J. S.
   *No. 1 in B Minor
   *No. 2 in A Minor
BEETHOVEN
   *No. 5 in F Major ('Spring')
   *No. 9 in A Major ('Kreutzer')

BRAHMS
   No. 1 in G Major
   *No. 3 in D Minor
CORELLI
   *No. 12 in D Minor ('La Follia')
FRANCK
   A Major

HANDEL	MOZART	TARTINI
*D Major	*C Major (K.296)	*G Minor ('Devil's Trill')
	*G. Major (K.301)	
	*E Minor (K.304)	

'Cello

BRAHMS	RACHMANINOFF
E Minor, Op. 38	G Minor, Op. 19
F Major, Op. 99	

SONGS

*BEETHOVEN
  ADELAIDE
*BRAHMS
  LULLABY
  SAPPHIC ODE
  MOONLIGHT
*DVORAK
  SONGS MY MOTHER TAUGHT ME
*FAURÊ
  CLAIR DE LUNE
*GRIEG
  I LOVE YOU
  A DREAM
  A SWAN
  FARMYARD SONG
*HAHN
  IF MY SONGS WERE ONLY WINGED
*MENDELSSOHN
  ON WINGS OF SONG
*SCHUBERT
  THE TROUT
  SERENADE
  GRETCHEN AT THE SPINNING WHEEL
  WHO IS SYLVIA?
  TO BE SUNG ON THE WATER
  WINTERREISE, DIE, song cycle

*SCHUMANN
  NUT TREE
  THE SANDMAN
  DEVOTION
  LIEDERKREIS, Op. 39
  DICHTERLIEBE, song cycle
  WOMAN'S LOVE AND LIFE, song cycle
*SIBELIUS
  BLACK ROSES
  WHISPER, O REED
*STRAUSS, R.
  SERENADE
  CRADLE SONG
  DREAM IN TWILIGHT
  TOMORROW
*TCHAIKOVSKY
  NONE BUT THE LONELY HEART
  WHY
*VAUGHAN WILLIAMS
  LINDEN LEA
  SILENT NOON
  ROADSIDE FIRE
*WOLF
  SECRECY
  THE GARDENER

SYMPHONIES

BEETHOVEN
  *No. 1 in C Major
  No. 2 in D Major
  *No. 3 in E Flat Major ('Eroica')
  No. 4 in B Flat Major
  *No. 5 in C Minor
  *No. 6 in F Major ('Pastoral')
  No. 7 in A Major
  No. 8 in F Major
  No. 9 in D Minor ('Choral')
BIZET
  No. 1 in C Major
BRAHMS
  Nos. 1 to 4
DVORAK
  *No. 5 in E Minor ('From the New World')
FRANCK
  D Minor
HAYDN
  *No. 22 in E Flat Major ('The Philosopher')
  No. 49 in F Minor ('Le Passione')
  No. 53 in D Major ('Imperial')
  No. 60 in C Major ('Il Distratto')
  *No. 83 in G Minor ('The Hen')
  No. 88 in G Major

  No. 92 in G Major ('Oxford')
  No. 96 in D Major ('Miracle')
  *No. 100 in G Major ('Military')
  *No. 101 in D Major ('The Clock')
  No. 103 in E Flat Major ('Drumroll')
  No. 104 in D Major ('London')
MENDELSSOHN
  No. 3 in A Minor ('Scotch')
  *No. 4 in A Major ('Italian')
MOZART
  *No. 25 in G Minor
  No. 31 in D Major ('Paris')
  *No. 35 in D Major ('Haffner')
  *No. 36 in C Major ('Linz')
  No. 39 in E Flat Major
  No. 40 in G Minor
  No. 41 in C Major
PROKOFIEFF
  *No. 1 in D Major ('Classical')
SCHUBERT
  *No. 8 in B Minor ('Unfinished')
TCHAIKOVSKY
  *No. 4 in F Minor
  *No. 5 in E Minor
  *No. 6 in B Minor ('Pathetique')

VARIATIONS

Orchestral

*ENIGMA VARIATIONS (*Elgar*)
*VARIATIONS ON A NURSERY SONG
  (*Dohnanyi*)
*RHAPSODY ON A THEME OF PAGANINI
  (*Rachmaninoff*)
VARIATIONS ON A THEME OF HAYDN
  (*Brahms*)

VARIATIONS SYMPHONIQUE (*Franck*)
SYMPHONIC VARIATIONS (*Dvorak*)
VARIATIONS ON A THEME OF FRANK
  BRIDGE (*Britten*)
*YOUNG PERSON'S GUIDE TO THE ORCHESTRA
  (*Purcell–Britten*)

Piano

*VARIATIONS ON 'ABEGG', Op. 1 (*Schumann*)
*VARIATIONS ON 'AH, VOUS DIRAIS JE'
  (*Mozart*)
*THEME AND VARIATIONS FOR PIANO FOUR
  HANDS (*Mozart*)

*ARIETTA IN A WITH 12 VARIATIONS
  (*Haydn*)
32 VARIATIONS IN C MINOR (*Beethoven*)
VARIATIONS ON A THEME OF PAGANINI
  (*Brahms*)

FOR THE YOUNG LISTENER

*Orchestral

'TOY' SYMPHONY (*Haydn*)
GREENSLEEVES (*Traditional*)
LARGO (*Handel*)
AIR from Suite in D (*Bach*)
SERENADE from Quartet No. 5 (*Haydn*)
ROSAMUNDE excerpts (*Schubert*)
CARNIVAL OF THE ANIMALS (*Saint-Saëns*)
PIZZICATO POLKA (*J. Strauss*)
VIENNESE WALTZES (*J. Strauss*)
INTERMEZZO from 'Cavalleria Rusticana'
  (*Mascagni*)

POMP AND CIRCUMSTANCE MARCHES
  Nos. 1 and 4 (*Elgar*)
COUNTRY DANCES (*Beethoven*)
COUNTRY DANCES (*Mozart*)
MILITARY MARCH No. 1 (*Schubert*)
MINUET (*Boccherini*)
A CHILDREN'S OVERTURE (*Quilter*)
PETER AND THE WOLF (*Prokofieff*)
YOUNG PERSON'S GUIDE TO THE ORCHESTRA
  (*Britten*)

*Piano

JESU, JOY OF MAN'S DESIRING (*Bach*)
FUR ELISE (*Beethoven*)
16 GERMAN DANCES, Op. 33 (*Schubert*)
DREAMING (*Schumann*)

GOLLYWOG'S CAKEWALK (*Debussy*)
FOR CHILDREN, based on Hungarian folk tunes
  (*Bartok*)

*Vocal

SANDMAN'S LULLABY and EVENING PRAYER,
  'Hansel and Gretel' (*Humperdinck*)

SEVEN NURSERY RHYMES (*Kabalevsky*)
SONGS FOR CHILDREN (*arr. William Clauson*)